REVISE EDEXCEL GCSE (9–1)

History

THE AMERICAN WEST, c1835–c1895

REVISION
GUIDE AND WORKBOOK

Series Consultant: Harry Smith

Author: Rob Bircher

A note from the publisher

In order to ensure that this resource offers high-quality support for the associated Pearson qualification, it has been through a review process by the awarding body. This process confirms that this resource fully covers the teaching and learning content of the specification or part of a specification at which it is aimed. It also confirms that it demonstrates an appropriate balance between the development of subject skills, knowledge and understanding, in addition to preparation for assessment.

Endorsement does not cover any guidance on assessment activities or processes (e.g. practice questions or advice on how to answer assessment questions), included in the resource nor does it prescribe any particular approach to the teaching or delivery of a related course.

While the publishers have made every attempt to ensure that advice on the qualification and its assessment is accurate, the official specification and associated assessment guidance materials are the only authoritative source of information and should always be referred to for definitive guidance.

Pearson examiners have not contributed to any sections in this resource relevant to examination papers for which they have responsibility.

Examiners will not use endorsed resources as a source of material for any assessment set by Pearson.

Endorsement of a resource does not mean that the resource is required to achieve this Pearson qualification, nor does it mean that it is the only suitable material available to support the qualification, and any resource lists produced by the awarding body shall include this and other appropriate resources.

For the full range of Pearson revision titles across KS2, KS3, GCSE, Functional Skills, AS/A Level and BTEC visit:
www.pearsonschools.co.uk/revise

\ Notes
* Flashcard

Contents

. . . .

A small bit of small print

Edexcel publishes Sample Assessment Material and the Specification on its website. This is the official content and this book should be used in conjunction with it. The questions in *Now try this* have been written to help you practise every topic in the book. Remember: the real exam questions may not look like this.

Plains Indians: social and tribal structures

Many different social and tribal structures made up the peoples known as the Plains Indians. Most tribes were divided into bands, each with a chief and a council. Examples of Plains Indians tribes include the Sioux, Cheyenne and Blackfoot.

1 Bands

Most people in a band were related to each other. Bands were led by chiefs and had councils of advisers. Council members agreed everything the band did. The survival and protection of the band as a whole was seen as more important than the individuals within it.

2 Chiefs

Chiefs were chosen because of their wisdom and skills as warriors/hunters. They were rarely chiefs for life. Chiefs and councils decided where their bands would go and what should happen to those who broke with customs and traditions. But they did not have to be obeyed.

3 Tribes

Bands in the same tribe supported each other during crises. Tribal meetings of all the bands were held each year to arrange marriages, trade horses and discuss issues. Chiefs and elders formed the tribal councils that advised tribal chiefs. Some tribes (e.g. the Sioux) were part of larger groups called nations.

4 Warrior societies

The best warriors from each band formed its warrior society. Members of the warrior societies supervised hunting and protected their bands from attack. All short raids and wars were led by the warrior society and the band's council would always consult them before they made decisions.

Chiefs and leadership

Plains Indian society did not view leadership in the same way as white American society did.

- No decision could be made until everyone at the council had agreed to it.
- The rest of the tribe or band did not have to obey the decision.
- Chiefs and elders were often guided by the spirit world through visions.

Chief Sitting Bull

Consequences: The US government thought that if a chief signed a treaty, all his tribe should obey the terms of the treaty, but this was not how Plains Indian society worked. For example, chief Red Cloud signed a treaty in 1868, but many Lakota Sioux bands followed chief Sitting Bull, who opposed it.

Band roles

A band saw every member as being equally important to its survival.

- Men (braves) hunted and fought enemies. Women (squaws) made clothing, fed the family and looked after their tipi.
- Everyone looked after children, who were taught the skills of their parents.
- Elders were respected for their wisdom but were left behind to die if their weakness threatened the survival of a band.

Consequences: Traditionally, Plains Indians children were taught by many different band members, and so when the US government tried to break Indian society up into family units, or when Indian children were moved to schools far away from their tribe, it meant Indian children did not learn all the skills and traditions of their people. This had an impact on Plains Indian ways of life.

Now try this

Explain the difference between bands and tribes.

Plains Indians: survival on the Plains

The Great Plains was a very tough environment: very dry, with very hot summers and extremely cold winters. Plains Indians depended on each other, the land and animals to survive. Plains Indians relied on horses to hunt, and the buffalo was considered the most important animal for hunting.

The importance of buffalo and horses

The Indians needed buffalo and horses to survive. Buffalo lived on the Plains. Horses had been introduced by Spanish invaders. The Indians bred and traded (or even stole) them.

Catching buffalo was quicker and easier on horseback.

Every part of a buffalo (except its heart, which was left on the Plain) was used for food, clothing and equipment.

The Indians believed a buffalo's heart gave new life to a herd.

Women and children cut up the buffalo meat. It was eaten raw or cooked. Some was stored for winter (known as jerky).

Indians could not live on the Plains without horses because they would not survive.

Wealth and status were measured by how many horses an Indian or tribe had.

Horses were used in war.

Horses carried the Indians and their belongings on their journey to find buffalo.

Some Plains Indians were nomads. They ate wild fruits and plants but did not settle long enough to grow crops.

Nomadic lifestyle

Most Plains Indians followed the buffalo migrations through the summer and autumn. They had a nomadic (travelling) lifestyle in these months.

- Tipis, made of wooden poles and covered in buffalo hide, were ideal for Plains life: their coned shape protected them against strong winds, flaps provided ventilation in the summer heat and they could be taken down and packed away in minutes.
- In winter, the bands moved to sheltered valleys where they lived in wooden lodges, insulated with thick layers of soil.

Consequences: Nomadic tribes found it very difficult to live permanently on reservations because they were used to travelling and hunting freely.

Bands and survival

Bands were designed for survival on the Plains. They changed size depending on the amount of food available. When food became scarce, bands would split up and spread out so that there was more chance of everyone getting enough to eat.

Consequences: Food was scarce on the Plains, so bands often moved outside their tribe's traditional hunting grounds and into areas controlled by other tribes. Sometimes this was done by treaty with other tribes. Sometimes it caused conflict.

Plains Indians constantly raided other tribes for food, horses and people. These raids were part of the way in which the tribes survived on the Plains.

Now try this

Explain **two** ways in which horses were important to Plains Indians.

Plains Indians: beliefs

Plains Indians' beliefs about nature and property, and their attitudes to war, had significant consequences for the relationship between Indians and white Americans.

Beliefs about nature

Plains Indians believed that:

- everything in nature had a spirit and that these spirits could help humans or harm them
- humans were a part of nature and should work with the spirits of nature, rather than try to tame and control nature
- they could contact the spirit world through visions and special ritual dances.

A Mandan Indian dance for successful buffalo hunting.

Beliefs about land and property

- Plains Indians tribes had sacred areas. For the Lakota Sioux, the Black Hills, Paha Sapa, were sacred because this was where the Lakota believed their tribe originally came from.
- Indian families sometimes had their own garden plots, but generally no one owned land. For Plains Indians, land was not any one's property, and not something that one person could buy and keep just for him or herself.

Consequences: White settlers had very different views about property from Plains Indians, which led to tension and conflict.

The Black Hills of South Dakota: the most sacred place of the Lakota Sioux.

Attitudes to war

- Plains Indian society was full of conflict, but Indians had developed ways to avoid too much killing because young men were essential to each tribe's survival.
- The highest respect and prestige was given to warriors, usually young men, for counting coup: landing a blow on an enemy and getting away without being injured.
- Indian war parties would also run away if a fight turned against them.

Any blow struck against an enemy counted as a coup.

Consequences: The US Army found it difficult to fight an enemy that ran away rather than fought to the last man. They had to develop new techniques against Indian warfare.

Now try this

Why was it important for Plains Indians to minimise the numbers of warriors killed in conflicts?

3

US government policy and the Plains Indians

The US government was keen to expand the USA westwards, but also believed it had to keep Indians and white Americans separate to avoid conflict.

Key events, 1830–1851

Timeline

1830 Indian Removal Act forces Indians in eastern states to move west of the Mississippi River.

The US government forced 46 000 eastern Indians to give up their lands in return for new lands **west of the Mississippi River**. Whites then thought this land was worthless – the 'Great American Desert'.

1834 Indian Trade and Intercourse Act sets out the frontier between the USA and Indian Territory.

A **permanent Indian frontier** divided Indian Territory from the eastern states. Forts guarded the frontier to stop whites crossing over to settle in Indian Territory.

1848 US victory in the Mexican–American War.

1851 Indian Appropriations Act: money allocated for setting up Indian **reservations** in modern day Oklahoma.

The situation changed when the USA gained new territories in the West. Instead of being on the western edge, Indian Territory was now sandwiched in the middle of the USA.

Government support for western expansion

- The government needed US citizens to go and live in its new territories in the West.
- This meant that people needed to be able to travel (on trails) across Indian lands.
- The US Army forced Indians to move away from trails in case Indians attacked travellers migrating from east to west.

Consequences: US policy started to change. The 'permanent' Indian frontier still marked the boundary with Indian lands, but now whites were allowed to cross the frontier.

The Indian Appropriation Act, 1851

By the 1850s, white Americans wanted to use parts of the lands in the West that had been given to Indians. Reservations were the solution. The government paid Indians to give up lands that whites wanted and move to smaller areas.

The Indian Appropriation Act paid for moving Indians in Indian Territory onto reservations. As well as keeping whites and Indians apart, the government hoped that reservations would help Indians learn to farm and live like white Americans. On reservations, white people could teach Indians about new ways of living. Reservations could become a way of controlling where Indians went and what they did.

Now try this

Why did the US government want Plains Indians to move to reservations?

Why move west?

You need to know the factors that encouraged migration to the West.

Pull factors for moving west

- 👍 Freedom and independence
- 👍 Fertile land
- 👍 Space
- 👍 Oregon Trail
- 👍 Gold

Push factors for moving west

- 👎 Collapse of wheat prices
- 👎 Overpopulation
- 👎 Persecution
- 👎 Unemployment

Timeline

Moving west

1825 Explorer Jedediah Smith shares discovery of the South Pass through the Rocky Mountains.

1836 The first migrants to travel the Oregon Trail by wagon reach their destination.

1837 Financial crisis causes economic depression: people lose savings, wages are cut and unemployment increases. Wheat prices fall; many farmers face ruin.

1841 Government-funded expedition maps the Oregon Trail and publishes guide book for migrants.

1846 Governor of Illinois tells Mormons to leave the state.

1848 Gold is discovered in California.

1858–59 Gold is discovered in the Rocky Mountains.

1874 Gold is discovered in the Black Hills (Dakota).

Financial panic in east USA

Boom years in the 1830s came to an end in 1837 with a financial crisis and a collapse in the price of cotton. Banks ran out of money, people lost their savings, businesses closed and many people lost their jobs. Unemployment reached 25% in some areas.

Farming crisis in the mid-west of the USA

In 1837, corn prices collapsed, leaving farmers facing ruin. This was not helped by overcrowding in this fertile farming region, in particular along the Mississippi valley. These were push factors for farmers to travel west.

Manifest Destiny

The US government needed to populate their territory in the West to defend it from foreign powers. This aim was reflected in the concept of Manifest Destiny: that it was God's will that white Americans should settle over all of America. White Americans at the time simply accepted that Manifest Destiny was right and natural.

> The key skill to develop for your period studies exam is being able to use what you know about the American West to explain **consequences** or **importance**, or in a **narrative account**.

Now try this

Explain **one** way in which government support was important in encouraging migration to the West in the 1830s and 1840s.

The Gold Rush of 1849

The discovery of gold in California in 1848 led to a huge increase in migration to the West, and also had significant consequences for law and order, settlement, farming and for the Plains Indians.

Who were the Gold Rush migrants?

From 1849, hundreds of thousands travelled to California, hoping to find gold.

- Between 1836 and 1846 the total number of migrants using the Trail was 5000. From 1849, tens of thousands used the Trail in the hope of finding gold in the West.

- Thousands more came by ship, from all over the world, to San Francisco. A famine in China led to 20000 Chinese people migrating to California in 1852.

- Most migrants did not find gold.

- Professional miners with the equipment and expertise to mine underground (where most of the gold was) took over through the 1850s.

Prospectors were people who looked for gold on the surface, especially in streams and river beds.

Consequences of the Gold Rush

Migration to California - 300000 people by 1855. California becomes a state.

Problems of lawlessness in the mining camps.

Farming boom in California.

Racial tension due to immigration.

Gold rush consequences

Manifest Destiny - White Americans see their 'destiny' coming true.

Gold from California boosts US economy - helps fund railroads.

Tension with Plain Indians due to huge increase in migration along Oregon Trail.

Genocide of Californian Indians by migrants.

Genocide is the deliberate killing of large numbers of people, usually because of their ethnicity. This definition fits the treatment of Californian Indians by white migrants.

Now try this

Using the diagram above to help you, explain **one** way in which the Gold Rush of 1849 was important for the development of the West.

You could focus on **one** of the following:

- The importance of the Gold Rush for the settlement of the West.
- The importance of the Gold Rush for relationships between whites and Indians.
- The importance of the Gold Rush for problems of law and order.

The Oregon Trail and the Donner Party

Those who migrated west had different experiences. There were set processes for following the Oregon Trail, to help protect migrants. The disasters of the Donner Party migration show what could happen when those processes were not followed.

The journey west

The journey west began at Independence, Missouri. Here, wagon trains (usually made up of 20 wagons or more) gathered for the trip, which took eight to nine months.

The Oregon Trail was 3200 km long – or 3800 km for those using it to go on to California.

Migrants needed to complete the journey before winter or risk getting stuck in the mountains.

Crossing the Great Plains was made dangerous by: sandstorms, quicksand, extreme heat, storms, disease, stampeding buffalo, hostile Indians and a lack of supplies.

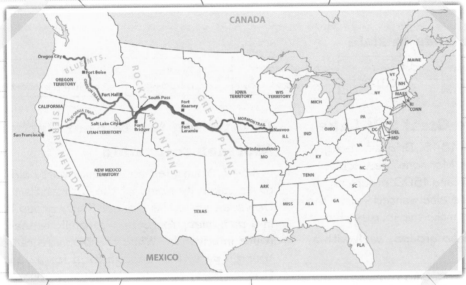

Migrants began the Trail in April when there would be enough grass for their animals.

Migrants needed to take enough food for the entire journey: a lot of salt pork!

Early migrants used explorers or Indians as guides; later ones relied on pamphlets.

Each trail crossed two mountain ranges: the Rockies, and either the Blue Mountains or the Sierra Nevada. They were steep, there was little to hunt, and the weather could be bad. Wagons were hauled across using chains, ropes and pulleys. Injuries were common.

The Donner party

The Donner party, led by Jacob and George Donner, left Missouri for California in May 1846 with 60 wagons and 300 people.

- This wagon train was well equipped but had more women, elderly people and children than normal.
- At Fort Bridger, a smaller group of about 80 people tried to take a 'short cut' (they were using a leaflet for guidance).
- Four wagons broke, 300 cattle died and one man killed another.
- They arrived late in the Sierra Nevada and were trapped by heavy snow.
- A group, sent for help, took 32 days to reach Johnson's Ranch.
- To survive, both groups ate their dead. Rescue parties found them in January 1847.

A 19th century woodcut of the stranded Donner party.

Now try this

Write a narrative account of the Donner Party migration, analysing why things went so badly wrong for the 'short cut' group.

Turn to pages 36–37 to find out more about writing narrative accounts.

The Mormon migration

The experience of the Mormon migration of 1846–47 shows how one group of migrants was able to deal with the challenges of migration through detailed organisation, religious motivation and hard work.

Joseph Smith

Smith founded the Church of Latter-Day Saints – whose followers are known as Mormons. His persuasive public speaking meant numbers grew to several hundred by 1830. He taught Mormons to obey him because he said his decisions were inspired by God. He was murdered in Illinois in 1844.

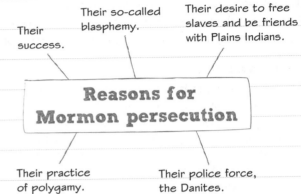

Reasons for Mormon persecution

- Their success.
- Their so-called blasphemy.
- Their desire to free slaves and be friends with Plains Indians.
- Their practice of polygamy.
- Their police force, the Danites.

Moving from state to state

New York State (1823-31) → Ohio (1831-37) → Missouri (1837-38) → Illinois (1838-46) → Utah (1847-present)

Journey to the Great Salt Lake

When Smith died in 1845, Brigham Young became leader. The Mormons' persecution in Illinois forced him and 1500 others to find land that no one else wanted – near the Great Salt Lake. To make the journey, he:

- split everyone into groups, each with a leader
- gave everyone a specific role
- taught them how to form their wagons into a circle for safety
- insisted on discipline and regular rest. His was the first of many Mormon wagon trains to make the 2250 km journey.

Comparing the Donner Party and the Mormon migration

In 1847, Young led an advance party along the route taken by some of the Donner Party in 1846. However, while the Donner Party group had trusted in a pamphlet, Young had carefully researched the route in advance. While the Donners ran out of food, Young's party had enough food for a year. While the Donner Party had many older and young people, Young's advance group of 150 was specially chosen with the skills to pick out the best route, improve the trail and mark out water sources and grass for the animals. All this prepared the way for the next wagon train of 1500 Mormons. Between 1847 and 1869, 70 000 Mormons followed the 'Mormon Trail'.

Why were the Mormons successful in Utah?

Their religious faith encouraged them to work very hard and prevented them giving up in the face of terrible hardship.

Brigham Young was in control and made good decisions.

The Mormon Church owned all land, water and timber, which were allocated to families. Towns ran efficiently.

Salt Lake City

They dug irrigation ditches which meant farm land had enough water.

A Perpetual Emigration Fund provided the resources to help thousands of Mormons to emigrate to Utah.

Young organised settlers so that each new town had the right mix of skills to survive and prosper.

Now try this

Identify **six** key events in the Mormon migration and connect them with sentences beginning like this:

As a result…   Because…   One consequence of this was that…   This led to…

Problems of farming the Plains

Settlers found many different problems in farming new lands in the West, but farming on the Plains was particularly challenging.

Climate - very hot, dry summers and very cold winters.

Grasshopper plagues and other insect pests.

Weather - thunderstorms and violent winds.

Lack of water - very little surface water and very low rainfall.

Problems of farming the Plains

Lack of trees - very little timber for fencing or building.

Prairie fires - dry grass burned easily.

Thick sod - the soil was a tangled mass of grass roots.

Dealing with a lack of timber

Due to a lack of trees to build with, settlers lived in caves and sod houses made from earth.

- The thick walls and roof were good insulation in winter.
- The earth walls and roof were fireproof, giving protection from prairie fires.
- However, sod houses were impossible to keep clean and were full of insects.

Sod houses were made from earth.

The lack of wood for fencing meant that settlers had to pay large amounts of money to import timber to fence their claims. This made homesteading expensive until 1874, when barbed wire was introduced as a cheap alternative to wooden fences.

A tough environment

The conditions for farming on the Plains were quite different from conditions in the East.

- Crops that did well in the East shrivelled up and died from lack of water, or were eaten by insect infestations, such as grasshopper swarms.

A Rocky Mountain grasshopper.

- Ploughs that worked in the East broke when farmers tried to use them to plough through the thick sod of the Plains.
- At first, settlers had to dig up the sod with spades, which was backbreaking work.

In California and Oregon, on the West coast, conditions for farming were much better. By the 1850s, Californian farmers were growing so much wheat they began exporting it worldwide.

Now try this

Explain why settlers on the Plains built houses out of sods or lived in caves.

The Fort Laramie Treaty, 1851

As the numbers of migrants using the Oregon Trail to cross Indian lands grew, tensions increased between white settlers and Plains Indians. Migrants demanded Army protection, which led to the Fort Laramie Treaty of 1851.

Reasons for tension between settlers and Plains Indians

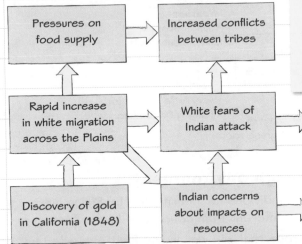

The huge increase in migrants along the Oregon Trail increased pressures on food supplies for Plains Indians, because the migrants disturbed the buffalo herds. Less food meant more conflicts between tribes. White migrants assumed that any Indian war parties they saw were a threat to them. Mostly, though, they were just witnessing conflict between tribes.

The significance of the Fort Laramie Treaty (1851)

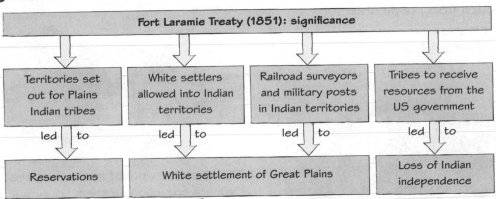

The Plains Indians tribes involved in the Treaty agreed to its terms in return for an annuity (yearly payment) of $50 000. This annuity became a lever for the US government to use against the Indians, and had the consequence of starting to encourage dependence of some Plains Indians on the government for food, resulting in a loss of Indian independence.

In the Fort Laramie Treaty, the US government prioritised the needs of white settlers over the previous commitments it had made about Indian lands in the Indian Trade and Intercourse Act of 1834. White settlement in the West increased because the Treaty allowed for safe passage of white settlers along the Oregon Trail. It also meant there was no longer a permanent Indian frontier between the eastern states of the USA and the Plains Indians. These changes allowed for the future possibility of reservations.

Now try this

Use the diagram above on the significance of the Fort Laramie Treaty (1851) to explain **two** consequences of the Treaty.

Lawlessness!

Lawlessness did not mean that there were no laws in the West, but that law enforcement was stretched too thin to make sure the law was being obeyed and that law-breakers were punished.

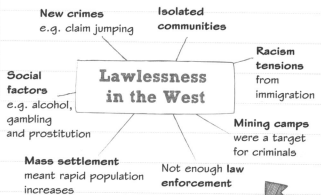

New crimes
e.g. claim jumping

Isolated communities

Racism tensions from immigration

Social factors
e.g. alcohol, gambling and prostitution

Lawlessness in the West

Mining camps were a target for criminals

Mass settlement meant rapid population increases

Not enough law enforcement

The main cause of lawlessness was such rapid rises in population that existing law enforcement could not cope.

Common issues

- Mining camps were usually isolated in the mountains, a long way from the reach of the law.

- Mining camps were almost all-male, and violence was fuelled by alcohol, bad luck at card games and fights over women.

- Prejudice against Chinese immigrants and other racism increased crime.

- Outlaws and conmen targeted miners who did make money, and swindled those who failed to strike it lucky.

- New crimes: claim jumping was when one man took over a promising claim made by someone else. Miners' courts were sometimes set up to help settle claims.

San Francisco gangs

- San Francisco's population grew rapidly with the Gold Rush: by 1849, it had grown from a small town of 1000 people to a population of 25 000.

- Very few prospectors found gold, and San Francisco quickly filled with unemployed, disappointed migrants.

- As more Chinese immigrants came to the city, racial tensions increased.

- By 1851, gangs had formed and were out of control in San Francisco. The few local policemen were unable to cope (and the gangs bribed many of them). Murder, violence and theft were commonplace.

- With no effective law enforcement available, citizens of San Francisco set up a vigilance committee to control the gang violence of 1851. The idea of vigilance committees spread to mining camps.

CHINESE GOLD MINING IN CALIFORNIA.

A famine in China led to a huge increase in Chinese immigration to San Francisco: 20 000 came in 1852. Chinese people were banned from working new claims, but even when their hard work meant they found gold overlooked by whites, whites would often steal it from them. Courts actively discriminated against Chinese people.

Key terms

 Vigilance committee (vigilantes) – a group of ordinary citizens that decides to punish suspected lawbreakers itself, instead of relying on the official justice system (usually because that system is inadequate).

Miners' courts – miners set up their own courts to settle disputes over claims. The camp usually selected a respected older miner to be the judge.

Now try this

Identify **two** ways in which local communities in the West tried to tackle lawlessness.

Sheriffs and marshals

The federal government (government of the whole USA) tried to tackle lawlessness in the West, but there were many problems to overcome.

US marshals
Appointed by the President to be responsible for a state or a territory. States and territories were very large so they needed deputies.

Deputy marshals
Assigned to specific towns and counties in the federal territories.

Town marshals
Appointed by townspeople on a yearly basis. Their job was to deal with local outbreaks of lawlessness, like saloon brawls and drunken shootings. They could appoint deputies if necessary. There were fewer town marshals than sheriffs but they did much the same work.

Sheriffs
Appointed in the counties for a two-year period of office. They could force local people to form into a posse to chase local lawbreakers. They could appoint deputies if necessary.

Federal control of law and order

- When a territory reached a population of 60 000, it could become a state with its own state legal system.
- Until it became a state, the federal government was in charge of the territory.
- The federal government decided on the laws for the territory and appointed a governor, three judges for court cases and a federal marshal (US marshal) for law enforcement.
- Once a territory had a population of 5000, communities could elect a sheriff. Sheriffs carried out law enforcement for a county.

Federal law and order problems

- Geography: territories were huge areas with scattered settlements. It would be days before news of trouble reached the US marshal, then days before any response could be made.
- The federal government did not spend much money on law enforcement, and law officers were poorly paid. This made corruption (e.g. taking bribes) much more likely.
- Sheriffs were mainly chosen for their ability to keep the peace (stop fights). They had no legal training and often their decisions were not very fair. This led to resentments.
- Settlers often disliked federal government and wanted nothing to do with its laws.

Now try this

Identify **two** ways in which the federal government tried to bring law and order to the West.

 'Identify' means you state the point: no need to describe or explain.

The Homestead Act, 1862

The Civil War was significant because it changed America and led to a new wave of settlement in the West. Post-war reconstruction was important. One consequence of the American Civil War was the Homestead Act of 1862. This provided incentives for people to take up unclaimed land in the West and build a new life there.

Before the American Civil War, the southern states blocked plans to give away family-sized farm plots in the West: they wanted to promote large plantation farms worked by slaves. When the southern states split from the USA (up until 1865), the Homestead Act could be passed into law.

Before the Civil War	US Civil War (1861 - 1865)	Homestead Act (1862)
North: small family farms and **no slavery. South: slavery** and large plantations.	Southern states leave the USA. Slavery abolished (1863).	Small family farms: 160 acres.

Could YOU be a homesteader?

Are you the head of a family or single and over 21 years of age?

(Women and former slaves ARE included – but no Indians and Confederate soldiers.)

Are you single and under 21 but fought for the victorious US Army in the Civil War?

Do you have $10 to pay to file your claim?

Then 160 acres of land is yours to claim.

Work the land for five years and it becomes your property for a further payment of $30.

Aims of the Homestead Act

The US government wanted to encourage the settlement of the West by individual family farmers. It did not want rich landowners buying up all the land in the West. That is why:

- the land was available very cheaply
- most American citizens (or would-be American citizens) could file a claim for land
- homesteaders had to be able to prove they had lived on the land and improved it
- homesteaders weren't allowed more than one claim.

Homestead Act (1862): consequences
Over **6 million acres** of federal land was homesteaded **by 1876.**
80 million acres was homesteaded by the end of the Act (1930s).
The promise of free land was an important pull factor for **immigration** to the USA.
Significant in encouraging white settlement of the **Plains:** especially **Nebraska:** half all settled land in Nebraska was homesteaded.

Limitations

🖓 There was a high dropout in homesteading: 60 per cent of claims were never 'proved up', often because of problems farming the Plains. The plots were too small for the dry Plains environment.

🖓 The government gave 300 million acres to railroad companies, who sold it to settlers. This was more influential than the Homestead Act in settling the West.

🖓 Despite the government's aims, rich landowners found lots of ways to buy up land using the Homestead Act.

Now try this

Explain **one** way in which the American Civil War was important in the settlement of the West.

The First Transcontinental Railroad, 1869

The Pacific Railroad Act (1862) provided the incentives for private companies to build the first transcontinental railroad (1869).

Why did the US government need railroads to connect the east and west coasts?

Railroads would enable troops to be moved around to control Indian uprisings.

Railroads would allow all Americans to keep in touch, creating national unity.

Railroads would help to fulfil white Americans' Manifest Destiny by making it easier to migrate and secure more areas of the country.

Railroads would let federal law officers reach new settlements that were having problems with law and order.

Railroads would promote the settlement of the West.

Railroads would transport goods to ports in Oregon and California, which were well positioned to trade with the Far East.

The Pacific Railroad Act (1862)

The southern states had blocked the proposed route of the first transcontinental railroad (Omaha to Sacramento) because it benefited the North, not the South. So, the Pacific Railroad Act could not be passed until the southern states temporarily left the Union in 1861.

The Pacific Railroad Act granted the enormous job of building the first transcontinental railroad to two companies: the **Union Pacific** and the **Central Pacific**.

Government support

There was massive federal financial support for the First Transcontinental Railroad:

- $61 million in loans ($16 000 for every mile of track laid; $48 000 per mile in the mountains)
- 45 million acres of free land for the railroad companies to sell to settlers.

The government also agreed treaties with Plains Indians along the route to move them away to new reservations.

The First Transcontinental Railroad was completed at Promontory Point, Utah, in 1869.

How did railroads promote settlement?

By 1880, the railroad companies had settled 200 million acres in the West.

- 👍 Railroad companies sold plots of land along their routes and set up towns at railheads.
- 👍 Railroad 'Bureaus of Immigration' sent agents to Europe to persuade immigrants to 'come West' and buy their land.
- 👍 The railroad companies used effective marketing to sell the idea of settling in the West.

Now try this

As part of the reconstruction that followed the Civil War, railroads were developed across America. Identify **three** impacts that railroads had on the development of the Plains.

Homesteaders: finding solutions

The period 1862–76 saw the development of different technological solutions to some of the problems of farming the Plains, as well as different farming methods. However, many of these solutions did not become widespread in the Plains until the 1880s and 1890s.

Problems	Explanation	Solutions
Lack of timber (not many trees on the Plains)	There was nothing to build houses with.	People built sod houses made from blocks of earth.
	There was nothing to make fences to contain cattle and protect crops from animals.	In 1874, Joseph Glidden invented barbed wire, which was quick and cheap to erect.
	There was nothing to use for cooking and heating.	Women collected dried buffalo and cattle dung, which was used for fuel.
Lack of water	There was low rainfall and few rivers and lakes.	Drills were developed to find underground water, then wind pumps built to bring it to the surface. 'Dry farming'
Hard, arid land (crops wouldn't grow)	Ploughs often broke going through deep-rooted grass.	Mass-produced and stronger machinery from eastern factories helped cultivate land more easily.
	Low rainfall prevented growth of crops like maize and wheat, which farmers were used to growing back east.	New techniques like dry farming (which conserved rainwater) were used. Migrants from Russia used Turkey Red wheat, which thrived on the Plains.
Natural disasters (prairie fires and pests destroyed crops)	Pests, such as grasshoppers, could destroy a whole season's crop. Fire spread quickly and burned everything.	There were no solutions. Homesteaders could be bankrupted by such disasters.
Land holdings were too small	The 160 acres allocated in the Homestead Act could not support the average family.	The Timber Culture Act 1873 let homesteaders have another 160 acres if they promised to plant trees on half of it. The Desert Land Act 1877 let settlers buy 640 acres of desert land cheaply.
Disease and lack of medical care (people were often ill)	Sod houses were hard to keep clean and had no sanitation.	Women cared for the sick, using their own remedies. As communities grew, doctors arrived.
Lack of education	Most homesteads were too far from towns with schools.	Women taught the young. As communities grew, single female teachers arrived and schools developed.
Isolation	Life was lonely and tough on the Plains.	Railroads improved travel and brought much-needed supplies to homesteaders. Communities worked together to build schools and churches. Women homesteaders formed valuable social networks.

Now try this

Explain how the Timber Culture Act (1873) aimed to reduce the problems of farming the Plains.

More problems for law and order

The Civil War and the railroads added to pressures on law and order in the West.

The impact of the Civil War

Wounded Civil War soldiers: the war made it difficult for many to fit back into 'regular' society.

The American Civil War had a significant impact on lawlessness in the West because:

- young men from the defeated southern states often resented the victorious US government and its laws
- large numbers of young men had been traumatised by the experience of the war and found it hard to fit in to 'regular' society
- the war devastated the South's economy, leaving many without jobs.

The impact of the railroads

The new towns created by the railroads in the West were known as **'Hell on Wheels'**.

- They often grew very quickly and had no local law enforcement.
- Some were 'cow towns', where cowboys, who had just been paid after weeks driving cattle, enjoyed drinking, dancing and fighting.
- 'Hell on Wheels' towns were notorious for gambling, heavy drinking and prostitution.
- Trains replaced stagecoaches for transporting valuables. This made them a target for train robbers.

A crowd greets the arrival of the Santa Fe Railroad to Kansas City in this movie still.

The Pinkertons were a private detective company. Banks, railroad and stagecoach companies employed Pinkerton detectives to track down robbers and thieves, as well as to provide general advice and protection.

Tackling lawlessness

The railroads and the electric telegraph improved communication between law officers, leading to an overall increase in federal government influence. However, new settlements were still mainly left to deal with lawlessness themselves, by electing sheriffs and town marshals.

- Cow towns often passed laws banning firearms.
- Sheriffs and marshals enforced these laws by force of personality (and often with their fists).
- Gangs of outlaws were sometimes too powerful to control and intimidated whole communities into supporting them.

Now try this

1 What does the importance of the Pinkertons suggest about lawlessness in the West?

2 Name **one** positive impact that the railroads had for law and order in the West.

Cattle trails and cow towns

The growth in the cattle industry after the Civil War occurred as railroads provided a way to move cattle worth $5 a head in Texas to the industrial cities of the North, which would pay $40 a head.

Quarantine laws block Texan cattle from Missouri (1855) and Kansas (1859).	Civil War - Texans fight for Confederacy. Cattle herds run wild: 5 million cows by 1865.	Beef in high demand in northern towns and cities. Drives to Sedalia blocked because of Texas fever.	Railroad reaches Abilene, Kansas. Joseph McCoy sets up first cow town. 35 000 cows driven to Abilene.	'Beef bonanza' - investors pile in to cattle industry from around the world. Rise of the cattle barons.
1855	1861-1865	1861-1865	1867	1870s

Farmers in Missouri and Kansas, where cows had no immunity to Texas fever, blocked the long drives to Sedalia and St Louis. Texas cattle were kept out of **quarantine zones**: the settled areas of Missouri and Kansas.

Texan cattlemen were desperate to find a way to get their cattle north and east to make big profits.

The long drives from Texas to the east had been happening since the 1830s. The big development was the railroad extending west.

Abilene, the first cow town

As the railroad moved further west, it created new **railheads** outside the quarantine zones. Joseph McCoy was the first to see the potential of Abilene, but it took work to make it a success, such as:

- building stockyards and hotels in Abilene
- building a new railroad spur for loading the cattle onto railroad trucks
- extending the Chisholm Trail up to Abilene, agreeing passage through Indian Territory
- promoting the new route in Texas – McCoy spent $5000 on marketing.

The Goodnight–Loving Trail

- Charles Goodnight and Oliver Loving realised there was another market for Texan cattle: new settlements in the West.
- The first trail, in 1866, was to Fort Sumner where the government had failed to get enough supplies for Navajo Indian reservations. 800 cattle sold for $12 000, which was four times the price of cattle in Texas.
- In 1868, Goodnight's trail extended up to Colorado (booming mining towns) and Wyoming, to the Union Pacific Railroad.
- Goodnight's success meant other cattlemen started to drive cattle to Wyoming, and Wyoming's cattle ranches began to grow.

Significance: Recognised new markets in West. Helped grow Wyoming cattle industry.

John Iliff and Plains ranching

- Iliff saw opportunities to sell meat to booming mining towns in Colorado.
- Denver, Colorado, was not on the railroad until 1870 and it was difficult to get supplies there – either over the Rockies or across the Plains.
- Iliff saw the opportunity to raise cattle on the Plains and began ranching near Denver in 1866.
- By 1870 he had a herd of 26 000 cattle on the Plains, on a ranch stretching over 16 000 acres.
- Iliff became Denver's first millionaire by selling his beef to miners, Indian reservations and railroad worker gangs.

Significance: First to raise cattle on the Plains. The start of ranching on the **open range** of the Great Plains.

Now try this

Cattle barons were rich, powerful men who controlled the cattle industry.

McCoy, Iliff and Goodnight were cattle barons. Explain why cattle barons were important in the growth of the cattle industry.

Changing roles for cowboys

Cowboys were often tough loners who worked hard and had a wild lifestyle.

What they wore

The hat (Stetson) gave protection from the sun, rain and cold.

The bandana, pulled over the nose and mouth, gave protection from dust when driving cattle.

A saddle was a cowboy's most important possession.

A lariat or lasso was used to catch cattle.

High-heeled boots meant their feet couldn't slip through stirrups.

Chaps protected cowboys' legs from vegetation and the weather.

Spurs were worn at all times.

Who were they?

Cowboys were mostly young single men. They were black American, Indian, Spanish and Mexican as well as white American. Many were former soldiers or drifters. Some were criminals on the run.

What were they like?

Cowboys were tough, hard-working and often hard-drinking. On long trails they could ride for between 12 and 24 hours a day in all weathers. Cowboys on the same cattle drive often worked miles apart, so life could be lonely.

A changing role

Cowboys on trails	Cowboys on ranches
Work was seasonal, from spring round-up to the long drive in the autumn.	Work was year-round and full-time, but fewer were needed.
Work included rounding up, branding and driving cattle hundreds of miles. They also looked out for sick and injured cattle. They started fast, then slowed to about 20 km a day for grazing.	Work included rounding up, branding and driving to market, but over much smaller distances. They also checked ranch boundaries, mended fences and looked out for sick and injured cattle.
Dangers included stampeding cattle, wild animals, crossing rivers and quicksand, rustlers, hostile Indians and extreme weather.	Dangers were fewer than on trails, but rustlers, wild animals and Indian attacks were still threats.
They slept in the open air and cooked on campfires.	They slept in bunkhouses and used cookhouses.
In their free time, cowboys might visit saloons and brothels in cow towns.	Drinking, gambling, guns and knives were banned. Many struggled to adapt to this lifestyle.

Now try this

List reasons why the role of cowboys changed between 1862 and 1876.

Ranchers vs homesteaders

As the development of the Plains increased, so too did rivalry over how the Plains were to be used. Ranchers needed a lot of public land, which homesteaders wanted to claim for themselves.

Ranching's reliance on public land

Open-range ranching needed a lot of land in order that large herds of cattle could roam around and have enough to eat. Federal law said everyone could pasture livestock on public land for free, and that is what the ranchers did. They divided up the open range between ranches and only bought a few plots here and there.

The problems came when homesteaders began filing claims to turn 160-acre plots of public land into homesteads.

Before homesteading

After homesteading

Blocking the homesteaders

Ranchers used different tactics to block homesteaders from taking up claims to 'their' public land. Three of these were:

1. Filing homestead claims themselves to all the parts of the range that homesteaders might be interested in.

2. Buying and fencing just enough land to block off access to other plots.

3. Taking homesteaders to court over rights to the land, knowing that homesteaders were too poor to pay court fees.

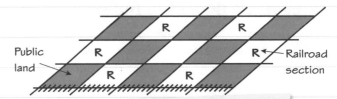

Railroad companies and public land were mixed in checkerboard sections.

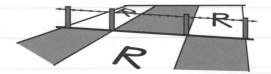

Ranchers bought railroad sections and fenced them to block access to public lands.

Fences make bad neighbours

As farming spread across the Plains, farmers and ranchers argued over fencing.

- Farmers said ranchers should fence their land to stop cattle roaming onto crops.

- Ranchers said their cattle had a right to roam; that fencing was the farmers' responsibility, and they should not harm their cattle.

- Arguments over fencing ended up in state court cases. Outside the courts, tension between ranchers and homesteaders was common. Sometimes this turned into open conflict.

Rivalry between cattlemen and sheep farmers led to range wars. Both sides relied on public land for grazing. Cattlemen used wire to fence off pasture, but sheep farmers cut the wire. Cattlemen led raids, killing hundreds of sheep.

Now try this

Explain why **one** consequence of the Homestead Act was conflict between ranchers and farmers.

Impacts on the Plains Indians

The expansion of the railroad, the growing cattle industry and gold prospecting all increased the pressures on Plains Indians' traditional way of life. The resources they depended on, which were already depleted, were shrinking as white America expanded from the east, west and south.

The impacts of railroads

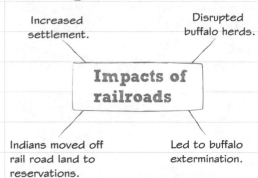

Increased settlement.

Disrupted buffalo herds.

Impacts of railroads

Indians moved off rail road land to reservations.

Led to buffalo extermination.

- Railroads disrupted the buffalo migrations through settled areas because of the noise of the trains and the fencing of railroad tracks. Railroads also contributed to the extermination of the buffalo.

- Railroads were funded by land grants that the railroad companies sold to settlers. Railroads encouraged settlement of the Plains.

- Railroads and reservations: the government persuaded tribes to give up lands along railroad routes and move to reservations.

Find out more about the extermination of the buffalo on page 30.

Impacts of the cattle industry

- Cattle and buffalo competed for the same grass, so, as cattle numbers increased, buffalo herds were put under pressure. The number of cattle in the West increased from 130 000, in 1860, to 4.5 million, in 1880.

- Cattle trails often crossed Indian lands. In Indian Territory, the tribes allowed this in return for a fee, but in the southwest the Comanche did not allow it and attacked cowboys, leading to tensions and US Army retaliation attacks.

Some Indians went to work in the cattle industry. Buffalo hunting skills were similar to skills for herding cattle on horseback.

Impacts of gold prospecting for the Plains Indians

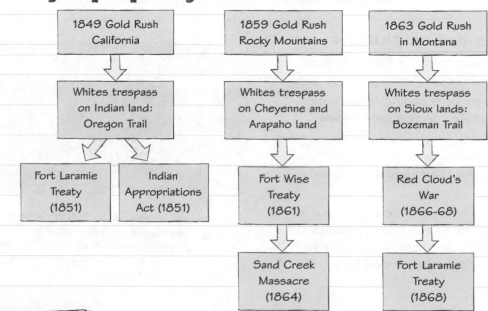

1849 Gold Rush California	1859 Gold Rush Rocky Mountains	1863 Gold Rush in Montana
Whites trespass on Indian land: Oregon Trail	Whites trespass on Cheyenne and Arapaho land	Whites trespass on Sioux lands: Bozeman Trail
Fort Laramie Treaty (1851) / Indian Appropriations Act (1851)	Fort Wise Treaty (1861)	Red Cloud's War (1866-68)
	Sand Creek Massacre (1864)	Fort Laramie Treaty (1868)

Use the diagram above to explain the impacts of gold prospecting for the Plains Indians.

Impacts of government policy

As more white Americans moved onto the Plains, the US government continued to move Indians onto reservations. The 1868 'Peace Policy' tried to manage the problems that this created.

Why did Indians move to reservations?

Usually because the tribe's council agreed it was necessary for survival.

- White American expansion meant there was less land to hunt on and fewer animals.
- The US government promised protection of their lands and regular supplies of food.
- Tribes desperate for food would sign treaties in order to get something to eat.
- Some tribes sided with the US government for support against their enemies.
- The US Army used force to move Indians to reservations and keep them there.

Impacts of reservations

Reservations undermined traditional Indian ways of life in three ways.

1 Reservations were made smaller, so that Indians could not survive by hunting. Many Indians became dependent on food supplies from the government (their annuities).

2 The Bureau of Indian Affairs agents that ran the reservations were frequently corrupt and cheated the tribes out of their annuities.

3 When conflicts arose because of these pressures, the government used them as an excuse to take more land from the tribes.

President Grant's Peace Policy (1868)

President Grant recognised that bad reservation management was leading to conflict. He:

- appointed new reservation agents, who had strong religious views (the idea being that these men would not cheat the Indians and would instruct them in Christianity)
- made an Indian, Ely Parker, the Commissioner of Indian Affairs
- obtained a budget of $2 million to improve conditions on reservations and create new reservations for all Indians.

Indians who resisted moving to reservations under the 'Peace Policy' were to be treated as 'hostile', and force could be used against them.

This cartoon from 1870 shows President Grant 'civilising' an Indian for votes and taxes.

Now try this

Explain why life on a reservation led to negative consequences for Indians' traditional ways of life.

The Indian Wars

Tensions between the Plains Indians and white Americans escalated into the 'Indian Wars'. The Fort Laramie Treaty (1868) was a temporary defeat in white America's conquering of the West.

1 Little Crow's War, 1862

Little Crow, a chief of the Santee Sioux Indians, lived on their reservation in Minnesota. In 1861, crops failed and food promised by the government didn't arrive – the Indians faced starvation. In August 1862, Little Crow and others attacked the agency that ran the reservation. They stole food to share, then burned the agency buildings. They also killed several US soldiers. By October, most Santee had surrendered or been captured. They were then moved to a smaller reservation, Crow Creek. Its barren landscape caused many deaths that winter.

2 The Sand Creek Massacre, 1864

The Cheyenne on the Sand Creek reservation were starving after crop failures. Led by their chief, Black Kettle, they attacked wagon trains and stole food but didn't harm travellers. After three years of attacks, Black Kettle negotiated with government officials and the army. On 29 November 1864, Colonel Chivington led a dawn raid on their camp. More than 150 Indians were massacred even though they waved white flags. Some, including Black Kettle, escaped and told other tribes what had happened. A US Senate Committee of Enquiry condemned Chivington. Both white men and Indians were horrified.

3 Red Cloud's War, 1866–68

Miner John Bozeman established the Bozeman Trail, connecting the Oregon Trail to gold in Montana. Bozeman's trail broke the Fort Laramie Treaty of 1851 because it crossed the hunting grounds of the Sioux. Red Cloud (a chief of the Lakota Sioux) led attacks on the trail travellers. In 1866, the government talked with him but he stormed out when he learned that two more forts were planned along the trail. In December 1866, Captain William Fetterman and 80 soldiers rode into a trap and were massacred by the Sioux, who blocked the route so no traveller could use it. The US army then negotiated a second Fort Laramie Treaty.

Red Cloud

The Fort Laramie Treaty, 1868

- US government agrees to abandon three forts and the Bozeman Trail.
- Red Cloud agrees to move his tribe to a reservation stretching from the Black Hills of Dakota to the Missouri River.
- Both parties are in favour of the treaty. However, the Indians, now split into reservations on separate sites, find it hard to act together.

Red Cloud was successful because he joined with other Sioux tribes led by Sitting Bull and Crazy Horse, plus some Arapaho and Cheyenne tribes. He managed to keep fighting through winter (not their custom).

Now try this

Explain why problems with the reservation system were important in causing the Indian Wars.

Changes in farming

During the period 1876–1895, new technologies and methods began to have a significant impact on farming the Plains. By the 1890s, the problems facing farmers in the West had become manageable.

New farming methods: dry farming

- Dry farming aimed to conserve the amount of water trapped in the soil: for example, by ploughing the soil immediately after it rained.
- Agricultural experts promoted dry farming as the best farming method for homesteaders to use in growing wheat.
- Dry farming was the main method responsible for turning the Plains into America's main wheat-producing region.

Dry farming methods were found to work well with the Turkey Red variety of wheat.

New technology: wind pumps

Wind pumps solved the problem of finding enough water to farm the Plains: now farmers could access water many hundreds of metres underground.

- Successful wind pumps in the West started with the development of a 'self-regulating' windmill: it turned automatically as the wind changed direction. It was invented in 1854, but it took years of development to become widespread.
- High steel towers, efficient gear mechanisms and large steel windmill blades were needed to generate enough power to pump water up from hundreds of metres underground.
- By the 1880s, powerful wind pumps had been developed that did not need constant repairing and oiling. These became widespread across the West.

New technology: barbed wire

- Barbed wire was first introduced in 1874 and became the ideal solution to the problem of there being no wood for fences.
- However, when it was first introduced it was relatively expensive and broke too easily. Some types had long barbs that wounded cattle.
- By the 1880s, a coating had been applied to the wire to make it stronger, and new techniques had made it much cheaper.
- As well as being used by farmers, the cattle industry used barbed wire to fence off land. Railroads used it to fence off tracks.

THE OLD WAY,   AND THE NEW.

Barbed wire had a significant influence on the development of the West.

Now try this

Turn to page 14 to remind yourself of the development of the First Transcontinental Railroad (1869).

Explain **one** way in which the spread of railroads helped the development of farming in the West.

Changes in the cattle industry

Through the 1870s, so much money went into cattle ranching that the open range became **overstocked**. This situation had several serious consequences for the cattle industry in the 1880s.

Consequences of overstocking the open range

Too many cattle
As cattlemen made more money, they bought and bred more cattle.

Overgrazing
There was too little grass, especially in the 1883 drought.

Prices dropped
An oversupply of beef meant prices dropped.

Less profit
Lower prices meant less profit. Some cattlemen sold up, others became bankrupt.

Winter of 1886-87
Freezing temperatures and deep snow meant at least 15% of cattle died. More cattlemen went bankrupt.

The end of the open range

After the winter of 1886, those cattle ranchers who were still in business moved to smaller ranches with fenced-in pastures.

- Smaller herds were easier to manage and could be brought under shelter in bad winter weather.

- Smaller herds in fenced pastured were easier to guard against cattle rustlers.

- Ranchers brought in high-quality breeds that produced better meat. These animals were kept separate from other breeds so their calves would be high quality, too.

- Smaller numbers of cattle reduced the supply of beef, which helped raise prices for beef again. Higher quality beef could also be sold at higher prices. This meant the cattle industry could start to recover.

Homesteaders often moved in to farm areas that had been used for open-range ranching. This also led to demands for surviving cattle ranches to fence their land to stop their animals from eating homestead crops.

Consequences for cowboys

Many cowboys also lost their lives in the winter of 1886–87, trying to find cattle in the deep snowdrifts of the open range. The end of the open range meant changes for cowboys, too.

Cowboys now had much less adventurous lives: branding, de-horning and dipping cattle, looking after horses and calves, mending barbed wire fences, repairing buildings, inspecting the grass in the fenced-off fields and harvesting the hay used to feed the herd during winter.

Cowboys lived in bunkhouses, which were often not very comfortable, with leaking roofs, thin walls and beds full of lice. There were schedules to keep to and rules to follow, which often included a ban on carrying firearms.

The smaller ranches only employed a few cowboys, so cowboy numbers dropped.

Now try this

What factors led to smaller ranches surviving the winter of 1886–87 better than larger ranches?

Continued settlement growth

In 1879, a migration of black Americans from the southern states to Kansas took place – the Exoduster movement. In 1889, the US government began to open up Indian Territory (present-day Oklahoma) to white settlers in a series of 'land rushes'.

The Exoduster movement and the Civil War

After slavery was abolished during the Civil War, black Americans in the southern states were supposed to become socially, politically and economically equal to whites. However, many white southerners prevented this. They kept their former slaves economically dependent on them and intimidated them with violence.

Continued **oppression** in the southern states.

Key individual: **Benjamin Singleton** promoted Kansas, helped migrants.

Kansas' reputation in the fight against slavery.

The **Bible** story of Exodus - an escape from slavery.

The Exoduster movement, 1879

The Homestead Act (1862) and the promise of free land.

In 1879 a **rumour** spread that the Federal government had given the whole state of Kansas to ex-slaves - this wasn't true but it was important in triggering the movement of **40 000** black Americans from the south states to Kansas and other western states.

Consequences of the Exoduster movement and Kansas (1879)

Problems with farming
- Other settlers had already taken the best land.
- Most Exodusters had no money for setting up farming.
- Most Exoduster homesteaders found it very difficult to survive.

Responses to Exodusters
- Southern whites strongly opposed the migration.
- Whites in Kansas did not think Exodusters should be helped.
- Kansas governor set up some help for migrants including some money to get started.

Consequences
- By 1880 mass migration ended: too many problems.
- By 1880 43 000 black Americans settled in Kansas.
- Exodusters typically stayed poorer than white migrants and had fewer rights.

The Oklahoma Land Rush

- Indian Territory had different sections for different tribes. In the middle was a section that wasn't allocated to any one tribe.

- Indian Territory was not open to white settlement. The US Army repeatedly had to move white settlers off the middle section.

- Then, in 1889, the US government opened up the middle section for white settlement.

- At midday on 22 April 1889, thousands of white settlers rushed over the boundary to claim their 160-acre section: a **land rush**.

The Oklahoma Land Rush of 1889.

There were seven Oklahoma land rushes in total. The first was in 1889, when 2 million acres were opened for settlement; the last was in 1895, when 88 000 acres opened for settlement. The largest Oklahoma Land Rush, the Cherokee Strip Land Rush, was in 1893, when 8 million acres were opened for settlement.

Now try this

Turn to page 8 to remind yourself of the details of the Mormon migration of 1846–47.

The Mormon migration and the Exoduster migration had similarities: both saw groups of migrants moving to the West to escape persecution. Both also had religious inspiration for the move.

What were the differences in the two migrations?

Billy the Kid and Wyatt Earp

The development of the West produced conflicts and tensions between people as they struggled to make a living. Billy the Kid and Wyatt Earp are both good examples of how these tensions affected lawlessness and attempts to enforce law and order.

Billy the Kid: a very brief history

- Billy grew up in poverty and was soon in trouble for stealing.

- In 1878, he became involved in a **range war** (Lincoln County War) between cattle baron John Chisum and smaller ranchers. Billy swore revenge when friends were killed.

- Billy's gang caused chaos across New Mexico – local law officers were also caught up in the range war.

- Only when a new governor appointed a new sheriff, Pat Garrett, could the law be enforced.

- After escaping jail, Billy was tracked down and shot dead by Garrett in 1881.

Conflict over resources: Billy involved in a war between ranchers.

Intimidation and corruption: local law enforcement was weak and caught up in the range war, too.

Geography: Billy's gang could easily escape the law and hide in remote areas.

Poverty: life for most people was hard. Being an outlaw was glamorous and exciting.

Billy the Kid

> While Billy the Kid and Wyatt Earp are examples of increased lawlessness at this time, it is important to remember that the general trend in the West was that law and order was getting more under control.

Wyatt Earp: a very brief history

- Earp first got into law enforcement after he was arrested for fighting in Wichita and then helped the deputy marshal deal with a rowdy bunch of cowboys.

- By 1879, he had moved to the mining town of Tombstone. Rich businessmen were fighting for control of the area with ranchers and cowboys led by the Clantons and McLaurys.

- In 1880, the businessmen hired Earp as deputy sheriff to end the fight in their favour.

- After months of clashes with the Clantons and McLaurys, Earp and his brothers killed two McLaurys and one Clanton at the OK Corral, on 26 October 1886. Cowboys then killed Morgan Earp. Wyatt Earp immediately killed two men who he said were responsible.

- Public opinion in the town turned against the Earps, who were considered murderers with no respect for the law. They left Tombstone in 1882.

Wyatt Earp and the OK Corral

Conflict over resources: Wyatt Earp and his brothers were involved in a war between businessmen and ranchers.

Intimidation and corruption: Earp and his brothers were accused of criminal acts (involvement in stagecoach robberies) and of murder – instead of reducing lawlessness in Tombstone, they increased it.

Wyatt Earp

Law and order: The gunfight at the OK Corral was criticised as lawlessness. Tombstone residents thought Wyatt should have arrested the suspects.

Unreliable lawmen: Earp was arrested nine times. Law officers often had criminal pasts.

Now try this

Do you think the cases of Billy the Kid and Wyatt Earp show that lawlessness was increasing in the West? Explain your answer.

The Johnson County War

Range wars were major conflicts for the control of land and resources in the West. The Johnson County War of 1892 is the best known. It was a conflict of cattle barons against homesteaders and small ranchers.

Background to the Johnson County War

The growth of the cattle industry in Wyoming
- Only 9000 US citizens lived in Wyoming Territory in the early 1870s.
- Most of the land was public.
- Huge cattle ranches developed, backed by foreign investment.
- A few very rich men owned the cattle ranches. They controlled Wyoming.

The impact of the winter of 1886-87
- The harsh winter caused terrible losses to the open ranch herds in Wyoming.
- The power and influence of the big ranchers was shaken, some went bankrupt.
- Smaller ranches did better as they could rescue more of the cattle.
- The big ranchers believed the smaller ranches stole cattle from them.

Tensions between big and small ranchers
- The population of Wyoming increased as more homesteaders and small ranchers moved there.
- By 1884, 10 000 acres had been homesteaded. Their barbed wire fences were a problem for the big ranches.
- The newcomers disliked the way the big ranchers would not share political power.
- In Johnson County, juries never convicted people accused of rustling big ranch cattle.

The killing of Ella Watson and Jim Averill
- Watson and Averill were homesteaders. Their 640 acre claim was to public land that rancher Albert Bothwell used for his cattle.
- Jim Averill wrote rude letters about Bothwell to the local newspaper.
- Ella Watson obtained a small herd of cows.
- Bothwell accused her of rustling his cows.
- Bothwell and his men hanged Watson and Averill and, soon after, took back the land.

The conflict begins

As a result of the killing of Ella Watson and Jim Averill, and three more murders, the small ranchers announced they would hold a **spring round up** of cattle earlier than the round up by WSGA (Wyoming Stock Growers Association): the big ranchers. WSGA members were sure the small ranchers would use this round up to steal more cattle from them.

The 'invasion'

- The WSGA hired 22 gunmen from Texas to 'invade' Johnson County and kill 70 suspected rustlers. They raised $100 000: most of it would be used to pay for legal costs after the invasion.
- The invasion failed. The 'invaders' got held up in a shoot-out with Nate Champion. Word reached Sheriff Angus of Johnson County, and residents of the county's main town, Buffalo. The invaders were surrounded and arrested.

The Johnson County 'invaders'

Consequences of the Johnson County War

- The WSGA's $100 000 was used to hire the best Chicago lawyers.
- The lawyers got the trial moved to Cheyenne. Juries here favoured the WSGA.
- The WSGA lawyers delayed the trial until Johnson County could no longer afford to keep the prisoners in jail.
- The state government, full of WSGA supporters, refused to help with the costs of the trial. The 'invaders' were set free.

Now try this

Why was it significant that the 'invaders' were arrested?
Why was it significant that they were freed?

Significance: Although the 'invaders' were set free, it is significant that vigilantism was so strongly resisted in Johnson County.

The Battle of the Little Big Horn, 1876

1876 was a turning point in the history of the American West because of the Battle of the Little Big Horn. In this battle, combined forces of the Sioux nation defeated the US Army. The shock of this defeat transformed US policy towards the Indians.

Key events of the 'Great Sioux War'

In the 1868 Fort Laramie Treaty, the Sioux were given a large reservation in South Dakota and could roam freely in the Black Hills (sacred for the Cheyenne, Arapaho and Sioux). Whites were not allowed to settle there or prospect for gold.

⬇

As the Northern Pacific Railroad got closer to Sioux land, General George Custer led cavalrymen to protect the railroad builders and look for gold. He found it!

⬇

Prospectors staked their claims to the land. The US government offered the Sioux $6 million for the Black Hills or $400000 a year for the mineral rights. They refused both offers and many bands left the Sioux reservation.

⬇

In December 1875, the Sioux were given 60 days to return to their reservation or be attacked. There was deep snow and it was impossible to travel.

⬇

By spring, over 7000 Indians were ready for war.

⬇

Sitting Bull, Crazy Horse and their people defeated General Crook at the Rosebud River on 17 June 1876. They then travelled west towards the Little Big Horn River.

⬇

On 25 June 1876, Custer attacked the Indian camp at the Little Big Horn. They were badly defeated - 225 men died and many were stripped, disfigured and scalped.

Custer's role

Some blame Custer for the army's defeat at the Battle of the Little Big Horn because:
- he should have waited for back-up (but if the Indians had spotted them, then he might have had no choice but to attack)
- he only had 600 men and split them to attack
- this meant they were heavily outnumbered and easily overcome (defeated).

Consequences of the Battle of the Little Big Horn

The massacre of General Custer and his men shocked and appalled most white Americans.

- Beforehand, public opinion favoured trying to reach agreement with the Indians.
- Afterwards, white people wanted to destroy the Indians, or at least their way of life.

Success or failure?

In the short term the Battle of the Little Big Horn was a huge failure for the US Army. However, because of the way in which they were defeated, some historians argue that it was actually a long-term success because the defeat led to:
- two forts being built and 2500 army reinforcements sent west
- the pursuit of the Cheyenne and Sioux until most were in their reservations
- the capture of Crazy Horse, who was later killed trying to escape
- Sitting Bull moving his tribes to Canada; however, food shortages forced his return and surrender in 1881
- the Sioux being forced to sell the Black Hills and other land, give up their weapons and horses, and live under military rule.

All of these were reasons for the Indians' eventual defeat.

Now try this

Identify the consequences of the Battle of the Little Big Horn for:
(a) reservations
(b) previous treaties with the Sioux
(c) continued resistance by the Sioux to the loss of their lands.

The Wounded Knee Massacre, 1890

By 1890, Indians on reservations were facing cuts in their rations, crop failures due to drought and despair at the loss of their lands and way of life. One response was the **Ghost Dance**.

The Ghost Dance

In 1890, Sioux rations were cut and a drought meant their crops failed. An Indian had a vision that if they all kept dancing, the Great Spirit would bring back the dead and a great flood would carry white people away. More and more Indians began to dance, which worried the Indian agents and white settlers. The army moved in to stop them.

Sitting Bull was killed when Sioux police tried to arrest him in case he led a new rebellion against the US control of his people.

His followers fled south to join the band of Big Foot, who had also fled when the army moved in.

The Wounded Knee Massacre, 29 December 1890

Snow and pneumonia slowed Big Foot's band down and the army caught them. They were taken to Wounded Knee Creek where the army began to disarm them. The Indians started dancing and shooting broke out. After ten minutes, 250 Indians (men, women and children) and 25 soldiers were dead. It was the end of Indian resistance.

The last clash between the Sioux and the US Army.

The end to Sioux bands resisting Army control.

Wounded Knee became a key symbol of oppression in the later fight for Indian civil rights.

Impacts of the Wounded Knee Massacre (1890)

The Massacre confirmed white views about the need to exterminate 'hostile' Indians. White people thought it was justified.

The end of the Indian frontier: nowhere within the USA now belonged to any other people or nation.

The end of the Ghost Dance: it had upset and worried white Americans, who saw it as a build up to trouble.

The end of the Plains Indians' way of life?

Factors leading to the end of Plains Indians' control over their way of life				
Railroads in the West	The extermination of the buffalo	The government's reservation policy	The discovery of gold in the West	Homesteads on the Plains

Now try this

Explain how the Ghost Dance contributed to the Wounded Knee Massacre.

Buffalo: hunting and extermination

Before the 1870s, white Americans had hunted buffalo for their warm coats, which were made into clothing. Removing and preparing the coat was a long, skilful procedure. In 1871, a process was discovered for cheaply and quickly turning buffalo hide into leather. Buffalo hunting became very profitable.

Source of life

In 1840 there were around 13 million buffalo on the Great Plains. By 1885 just 200 survived. Buffalo provided Plains Indians with almost all they needed to survive. Their destruction meant the destruction of this way of life.

Buffalo Bill

William Cody was employed by the Kansas Pacific Railroad Company to clear buffalo from the tracks and supply workers with meat. He claimed he had killed 4280 buffalo in 17 months – hence his nickname.

How buffalo were exterminated

Their habitat was crossed by railroads. Railroad companies used hunters to kill them to feed construction workers.

They were killed by tourists. Special excursion trains brought people onto the Plains to hunt them for sport.

Their hides were made into quality leather goods. White hunters earned good money supplying them.

The grassland they fed on was destroyed or eaten by other animals when settlers built houses, towns, trails and railroads. They also caught diseases spread by the settlers' cattle and horses.

Who was responsible?

Some people suspected that the government encouraged the destruction of buffalo to control the Indians.

- Early on, Indians could leave reservations to hunt, but this was banned in the late 1860s to encourage Indians to live like white people.
- Destroying the buffalo meant Indians were less likely to protest about the loss of their nomadic lifestyle.

- Neither the government nor the army did anything to stop the destruction. In fact, they seem to have encouraged it.
- White Americans enjoyed buffalo hunting and the wealth that hides brought them.

Now try this

Give **five** examples of ways in which white Americans destroyed the buffalo.

Life on the reservations

Reservations cut down Indian lands into scraps of territory. Different methods were used to destroy Indian identities, with the aim that Indians would stop resisting the spread of 'civilisation' and join in the white American way of life instead.

Reservation land
Indian reservations were created on land that was least wanted by white Americans. It was not fertile, didn't contain minerals and would make survival difficult.

Indian agents
The government appointed Indian agents to look after the reservations, but they were often corrupt. Money or rations intended for the Indians often disappeared.

Life on reservations

Living conditions
Rations were poor and crops often failed. Medical care was very poor. Diseases such as measles and 'flu' were common. Many reservation Indians died from them.

Indian Agency Police
Some Indians joined this force to control reservations. In return, they had better food, clothing and shelter than others on the reservation.

1 Tribal chiefs lost their power

The government slowly removed the ability of chiefs to influence and guide their bands and tribes.

- 1871: chiefs no longer signed treaties.
- Early 1880s: chiefs no longer looked after reservations, councils did.
- 1883: Indians were judged and punished in special courts. These were abolished in 1885 and replaced with US federal law courts.

2 Indian children were taught white American values

They were sent to schools where they were punished for using their own language and respecting their culture. They no longer fitted in with their families, but they weren't accepted by the whites, either.

4 Indian beliefs were banned

Putting an end to feasts, dances and ceremonies reduced the power of medicine men, who were an important part of Indian life. Christian missionaries were sent in to 'civilise' the Indians.

3 Indians were not allowed to hunt

This affected their whole social structure and removed men's traditional role. It also affected their clothing and lifestyle.

5 Indians were de-skilled

They were excellent horsemen, hunters and warriors. However, they had no horses on reservations, so they could not hunt buffalo or fight. Some Indians refused to learn 'white' skills like ploughing, sowing and reaping.

Now try this

Explain **two** reasons why reservations led to Indian tribes losing their independence and having to rely more and more on the federal government for food and clothing.

Changing government attitudes

The reservation system had been designed to help Indians assimilate into white America, as well as to prevent them from getting in the way of the white takeover of the West. However, by the 1880s, the reservation system was seen as encouraging Indians to depend on government handouts.

Pressures on government policy

Government policy swung between assimilation and protection.

Assimilation = becoming part of US society.

Indians should assimilate into white America:
- become farmers
- become Christians
- settle in one place.

Pressure from whites wanting Indian land – for minerals, for farming.

Government attitudes to the Plains Indians

Indians should be protected from whites:
- protected land
- treaties
- government support.

Pressure from whites who thought Indians were being given too much help.

The Dawes Act, 1887

- Each Indian family was allotted a 160-acre share of reservation land: a homestead plot.
- 80 acres were allotted to single Indians; 40 acres to orphans under 18.
- Indians who took their allotment and left the reservation could then become American citizens.
- Indians could not sell their land allotments for 25 years.
- All the reservation land left over after the allotments could be sold to whites.

Encourage individualism instead of tribal identity.

Encourage individual Indians to assimilate and become US citizens.

Reduce the influence of chiefs and the tribal council.

Aims of the Dawes Act (1887)

Encourage Indian families to farm for themselves, not rely on the tribe.

Free up more land for white settlers.

Reduce the cost of running the reservation system for the US government.

The significance of the Dawes Act

The Act failed to improve conditions for Indians.

- By 1890, Indians had lost half the lands they had had in 1887 to whites.
- Indians who took up allotments were not able to farm successfully: the land was too poor and they didn't have enough land for the dry conditions.
- Most Indians sold their land as soon as they could, and ended up landless.
- White Americans cheated many Indians into selling their land.

The closure of the Indian Frontier

In 1890, the US census office, part of the US government, declared that there was no longer a frontier line between white settlement and 'wilderness' (Indian lands). The USA had complete control of the West.

Now try this

Explain why many white Americans thought Indians should assimilate into their way of life.

Exam overview

This page introduces you to the main features and requirements of the Paper 2 Option 24/25 exam paper.

About Paper 2

- Paper 2 is for both your period study and your British depth study.
- The American West, c1835-c1895 is a period study – it will be in Section A of Paper 2.
- You will answer all the questions in Section A. In question 3, you pick two statements to explain out of a choice of three.

> Remember to read each question carefully before you start to answer it.

> The Paper 2 exam lasts for 1 hour 45 minutes (105 minutes) in total. There are 32 marks for this period study and 32 marks for the British depth study, so you should spend about 50 minutes on each.

The three questions

The three questions for The American West will always follow this pattern.

Question 1

Explain **two** consequences of...   (**8 marks**)

> Question 1 targets both AO1 and AO2. This question focuses on consequences – things that happened as a result of something.

> Four of these marks are for Assessment Objective 1 (AO1). This is where you show your knowledge and understanding of the key features and characteristics.

> Four of these marks are for Assessment Objective 2 (AO2). This is where you explain and analyse key events using historical concepts, which, in this case, is consequence.

Question 2

Write a narrative account analysing...   (**8 marks**)

Two prompts and your own information.

> Question 2 also targets both AO1 and AO2. It asks you to provide an analytical narrative – an analysis of causation, consequence or change.

Question 3

Explain **two** of the following...   (**16 marks**)

Three statements each starting:
The importance of... for...

> Question 3 targets both AO1 and AO2 and asks you to provide an analysis of consequence and significance – 'how important'.

> You can see examples of all three questions on pages 34–39 of this Skills section, and in the Practice section on pages 40–49.

Question 1: Explaining consequences 1

Question 1 on your exam paper will ask you to 'Explain **two** consequences of...'. There are 8 marks available for this question: 4 for each consequence.

Worked example

Explain **two** consequences of the Dawes Act (1887).   **(8 marks)**

What is a consequence?

A consequence is something that happens as a result of an event.
You can help yourself to 'think consequences' by using phrases such as:

- 'As a result of...'   • 'This meant that...'
- 'This allowed...'   • 'This led to...'

🔗 Links You can revise the Dawes Act on page 32.

Sample answer

Consequence 1:

Indians lost even more land.

Consequence 2:

The Dawes Act encouraged Indians to learn farming because the US government wanted Indians to become self-sufficient.

This is a correct consequence of the Dawes Act, but make sure your answer explains why it was a consequence (AO2), or adds specific information to support the answer (AO1).

This is not a consequence but a **reason for** the introduction of the Dawes Act. Remember, for the Section A exam it is essential to think **results of** not reasons for.

Improved answer

Consequence 1:

By 1890, Indians had lost half their 1887 lands to white settlers. This was the result of the provision in the Dawes Act that reservation land not allocated to Indian families or individuals could be sold to non-Indians. Also, although the Dawes Act prevented Indians selling their allotted land for 25 years, many Indians were still cheated into selling it for a cheap price.

You need to explain how the consequence of loss of lands resulted from the Dawes Act, and also include relevant information from the period to support your answer: in this case, figures about land loss and specific details from the Dawes Act.

Consequence 2:

Although the Dawes Act had aimed to encourage Indians to take up farming, most Indian families who tried to farm their plots could not feed themselves this way. This was a result of reservation land being generally poor land for farming, and a consequence of most Plains Indian tribes having no tradition of farming. 160 acres had also already proved to be too small an area for farming the Plains, but the Dawes Act still only gave a maximum of 160 acres to each Indian family.

Note how the student has changed this from an explanation of an aim into the analysis of a consequence. Notice how the student has used the phrase 'This was a result of...' to focus the answer on consequences. Make sure your answer explains how problems with the Dawes Act led to these consequences.

Question 1: Explaining consequences 2

Read carefully through this second Question 1 example and the student answers. The hints and tips on this page apply to all Question 1 questions, as do the ones on the previous page.

Explaining consequences

Consequences = results of.
For consequences, think: 'What happened as a result of...?'
To explain consequences, you must show the **connection** between the key event and the consequence.

Worked example

Explain **two** consequences of the introduction of barbed wire (1874).   **(8 marks)**

 **Links** You can revise the introduction of barbed wire on page 23.

Sample answer

Consequence 1:

On the Plains there weren't many trees and so homesteaders were not able to fence their crops, but when barbed wire was invented they could fence their crops.

 This is a correct consequence but the student has only given a vague answer. Make sure you explain the consequence in your answer.

Consequence 2:

Fights between ranchers and homesteaders happened because of barbed wire, because homesteaders fenced off the open range.

 Notice how this is also a correct consequence and the beginning of an explanation: you would need to add more detail to the explanation to improve this answer.

Improved answer

Consequence 1:

On the Plains there weren't many trees and this meant homesteaders had no timber to fence their claims, which was a problem as they couldn't protect crops from wandering livestock, or protect their own livestock. Barbed wire allowed homesteaders to build effective fences. Purchasing timber to make fences was very expensive, yet barbed wire quickly became very cheap – just 2 cents per pound of wire by the 1880s. The barbs were effective at keeping livestock away so homesteader crops were safe from livestock.

 You should identify what the situation was like **before** the introduction of barbed wire, as this will help you to explain the consequence that followed its introduction.

 Use your knowledge of the period to support your answer.

 State the consequence and **explain** how that consequence resulted from barbed wire being introduced in the West.

Consequence 2:

Homesteaders used barbed wire to fence off waterholes on their land, which they relied on for water for their families, crops and livestock. In the 1870s, cattle ranchers often relied on their cattle being able to use the same waterholes on trails or as they roamed on the range. One consequence of this was conflict between the ranchers and homesteaders. The ranchers would cut barbed wire and let their cattle through because they had been using the waterhole for longer than the homesteaders.

 Links The information about the cattle industry in the 1870s is useful for providing context. Revise the early cattle industry on pages 17–19.

 You can say 'One consequence of this...' to make your answer clear.

 You could also include some information about homesteaders' responses to the introduction to barbed wire.

Question 2: Analytical narrative 1

Question 2 on your exam paper will ask you to 'Write a narrative account analysing...'. A narrative account explains how events led to an outcome. There are 8 marks available for this question.

Worked example

Write a narrative account analysing the ways in which migration to the West grew in the years 1836–1850. **(8 marks)**

You may use the following in your answer:

• The setting up of the Oregon Trail (1836).
• Economic problems in the East.

You **must** also use information of your own.

Analytical narrative

A narrative sounds like it means 'Tell the story of...', but this is **not** what you need to do for this type of question.

The 'analytical' bit means you have to consider how key events were connected. Like all the questions on this paper, you need to think about **consequences** and **causes**: what happened as a result of a key event.

Links You can revise migration to the West on pages 5–9.

Sample answer

It was possible to travel to Oregon and California by ship, but the journey was very expensive ($500) and took a year. In 1836, a missionary family were the first people to travel overland to Oregon by wagon along the Oregon Trail. Migrants needed wagons to carry everything they needed to set up new lives in the West, so the opening of the Oregon Trail was significant.

Travelling the Oregon Trail was cheaper and faster than travelling by ship: it took six months, starting from Independence, Missouri. As a result, when the effects of the 1837 financial crisis hit the East of the USA, the Oregon Trail provided a reliable and affordable route West. Following a government survey of the route, guides to the Trail were published, which meant that migrants could prepare for the journey. In 1843, a wagon train of 900 people successfully made the trip. People suffering from high unemployment in the East were inspired to migrate by these successes.

The increase in migration, from 1000 people a year in 1843 to 300 000 in 1849, was the result of the California Gold Rush. People travelled from all over the world in the hope of getting rich. Many tens of thousands travelled there across the Rocky Mountains and Sierra Nevada, along the Oregon and California Trails. Without the Trails, migration to the West would have been a very different story.

Key events

Your first step in writing an analytical narrative is to identify the key events in your narrative. This answer has selected the setting up of the Oregon Trail (1836), financial crisis in the East (1837), publication of surveys and guides to the Oregon Trail and the California Gold Rush (1849).

Creating links

Once you have identified the key events, your answer should consider how one key event links to the next. This answer has signposted this with phrases such as 'As a result...' and '...which meant that...'.

Information of your own

The question states that you may use the two prompts it provides (the two bullet points), but also that 'You must also use information of your own'. Make sure you do use your own information as the best answers do this. In this answer, the student has included their own information about the Gold Rush, government surveys and publications of guides.

Logical structure

If you plan your answer by noting down your key events first on scrap paper, this will help you structure your answer into a clear and logical sequence. Start with the earliest key event and work from one event to the next, identifying consequences, causes and changes.

Question 2: Analytical narrative 2

Read carefully through this second Question 2 example and the student answers. The hints and tips on this page apply to all Question 2 questions, as do the ones on the previous page.

Worked example

Write a narrative account analysing the destruction of the buffalo herds by 1883.

(8 marks)

You may use the following in your answer:

- Extermination of the southern herd (1874).
- The breakup of the Great Sioux reservation (1876).

You **must** also use information of your own.

More on analytical narrative

Question 2 asks you to explain how events led to an outcome. Identifying the events that were involved and showing how they led to the outcome provides the analysis. Showing how one event led to another event, or was linked to existing circumstances, provides the narrative. That's what makes it analytical narrative.

 Links You can revise the destruction of the buffalo herds on page 30.

Sample extract

The Plains Indian lifestyle depended on the buffalo. So, the impact of the destruction of the buffalo herds by 1883 was very severe on the Plains Indians. Various factors were involved in the destruction of the herds, including Indian hunting of the buffalo, industrial processes that used buffalo hide for leather and the extension of the railroad network over the Plains. The railroads brought the hunters to the Plains and also took away the buffalo hides.

Instead of providing an analytical narrative, this is a jumble of points about the extermination of the buffalo. Remember: you need to **identify the key events** that led to the outcome (the extermination of the buffalo), and then **link them together in a logical sequence.**

Improved extract

Before the 1870s, buffalos were hunted by whites for their dense winter coats, which were made into very warm items of clothing. It took a lot of skill to remove the coat and to process it, and hunters only hunted in winter. This reduced the impact of white hunting on the herds.

In 1871, however, a process was discovered for quickly and cheaply turning buffalo hide into leather. Leather was in great demand in the industrial cities of the USA, not least because it was used for the machine belts used to power many of the manufacturing machines. The price for buffalo hides rose quickly, to as much as $3 per hide. People travelled by railroad to the southern Plains, armed with the new Sharps hunting rifle, and, between 1872 and 1874, professional hunters killed 4.5 million buffalo.

The northern herd was protected by the Great Sioux reservation until 1876…

Here is the first part of the student's improved answer. Note how the answer is set out in chronological order. This sequence makes it much easier to show how each key event links to the next.

The student has used their knowledge to identify why the previous market for buffalo coats did not have the same impact as the market for buffalo leather. Using your knowledge in this way will help your analysis.

Although the answer selects good key events for its analytical narrative, the student could have made more use of 'process' words and phrases. Remember to use these to show how one event led to another. For example: '**Because** of the good money to be made from buffalo hides, people travelled by railroad…'; '**As a result** of this combination of high demand for hides, railroads and high-powered, highly accurate hunting rifles, professional hunters killed…'

Question 3: Explaining importance 1

Question 3 provides three statements about the **importance** of events and developments, and asks you to pick two of them and **explain** why they were important. There are 16 marks available for this question: 8 marks for each explanation.

Worked example

Explain **two** of the following:

[✗] The importance of the Pacific Railroad Act of 1862 for the settlement of the West.

[ ] The importance of the Timber Culture Act of 1873 for the development of settlement in the West.

[ ] The importance of Abilene's establishment as a cow town (1867) for the growth of the cattle industry. **(16 marks)**

Choosing which point to answer

Although three bullet points are listed, the question only asks you to pick **two** of them for your answer: you should pick the two you can answer best and write two separate answers for this question.

Pay careful attention to what exactly you are being asked to explain: the second part of each bullet point gives you the specific focus of the question.

Links You can revise these events on pages 14, 15 and 17.

Sample extract

The Pacific Railroad Act of 1862 provided the stimulus for private companies to build the First Transcontinental Railroad, which was completed in 1869. The Pacific Railroad Act split the job of building the 2000 km railroad between two companies: the Union Pacific and the Central Pacific. No railroad company would have taken the risk of building the railroad without the support provided by the US government, which loaned each company $16 000 for every mile of track they laid ($48 000 per mile for mountain areas) and granted each company huge areas of public land along the route to sell.

On the exam paper, put a cross in the box to show which question you are answering. This is the first part of an answer to the first question.

Although the student includes accurate and relevant detail about the Pacific Railroad Act, notice how they do not show any analysis of its importance. When answering a question such as this, think first about the reasons why the Pacific Railroad Act helped the settlement of the West, and then use your knowledge about the period to support your analysis.

The best answers show analysis of importance (AO2) together with detail (AO1).

In order to improve their answer, the student spent two minutes planning it before they started to write. This is what they did:

| Government money meant First Transcontinental Railroad could be built. | Government wanted railroads to achieve Manifest Destiny - settlement for the West. | Government agreed treaties with Indians to move away from the railroad route - allowing settlement. |

Importance of the Pacific Railroad Act for settlement

| Act granted land to railroads to sell to settlers. Importance of railroads in supporting settlement. | Act also = electric telegraph along route of railroad: increased communication for settlers and law and order. |

Planning your answer makes a lot of sense, because it helps you to focus on the demands of the question. Also, you can structure your answer and it helps you to plan your time. But make sure it is a quick plan that allows you plenty of time to write your answer.

You can see part of the improved answer that the student wrote using this plan on the next page.

Don't forget that you need to write answers for **two** parts of the question!

Question 3: Explaining importance 2

This student answer is an improved version of the student answer from the previous page. The hints and tips on this page apply to all Question 3 questions, as do the ones on the previous page.

Worked example

Explain **two** of the following:

[✗] The importance of the Pacific Railroad Act of 1862 for the settlement of the West.

[ ] The importance of the Timber Culture Act of 1873 for the development of settlement in the West.

[ ] The importance of Abilene's establishment as a cow town (1867) for the growth of the cattle industry.   **(16 marks)**

 You can revise these events on pages 14, 15 and 17.

Importance and significance

Question 3 tests your ability to explain how and why an event is significant. A strong answer would explain two or three consequences of the event and contain relevant factual knowledge. The best answers will also be organised and flow smoothly, something you can achieve by using 'linking' phrases, such as 'It was also important because it led to...', or, 'Thirdly, it meant that...'.

Improved extract

The Pacific Railroad Act provided the money and incentives for the First Transcontinental Railroad to be built, between 1863 and 1869. In 1869, the flow of migrants along the Oregon Trail began to dry up as people chose instead to make the quicker, safer, cheaper and more comfortable journey West by rail. The Pacific Railroad Act provided a better route for settlers to get to the West. The government had passed the Act in order to achieve the USA's Manifest Destiny and it knew how important the railroads would be to achieving that.

In order to incentivise the two railroad construction companies to build the First Transcontinental Railroad, the Pacific Railroad Act enabled huge loans of money to be made, and also for the US government to grant the companies 45 million acres of public land, which they could sell at a profit. These land grants, along the route of the railroad, were very important in the settlement of the West. Railroad companies promoted their land all over the USA and Europe and were responsible for selling far more land for settlement in the West than the Homestead Act achieved.

The Pacific Railroad Act also meant the government agreed treaties with Indian tribes (for example the Pawnee) along the route of the First Transcontinental Railroad, so that the Indians gave up their lands and moved away from the route to new reservations. This was also important because it opened up these areas for settlement by whites.

The student has used their plan (see previous page) to structure their answer. Notice how the student often starts a new paragraph when moving onto a new reason for the importance of the Pacific Railroad Act.

 The student backs up the reason why the Act was important with specific information. For example, here it is the information about the decline in migrants using the Oregon Trail.

 It is easy, when writing answers to questions like this, to start to drift away from the event in the question (the Pacific Railroad Act) and talk about railroads in general. Notice how the student does not do that: they keep the focus on the Pacific Railroad Act and its importance.

 Notice how the student again uses relevant information to support their points here.

 It is useful to compare the importance of the Pacific Railroad Act with other events that were factors in the development of settling: the Homestead Act, in this case.

 The student has not really developed this final point, perhaps because of a lack of time. They do explain importance, but it would have been good to have developed the point and supported it with relevant information.

Practice

Put your skills and knowledge into practice with the following question.

Option 24/25: The American West, c1835–c1895

1 Explain **two** consequences of Red Cloud's War (1866–68).

(8 marks)

Consequence 1:

....

....

....

....

....

....

....

....

....

....

....

....

Consequence 2:

....

....

....

....

....

....

....

....

....

....

....

You have 1 hour 45 minutes for the **whole** of Paper 2, so you should spend about **50 minutes** on Option 24/25: The American West, c1835–c1895. Remember to leave 5 minutes or so to check your work when you've finished writing.

Links You can revise Red Cloud's War on page 22.

You need to identify **two** valid consequences and support each one.

Your exam paper will have a separate space for each consequence you need to describe.

Remember to include **two** consequences in your answer and to spend equal time on both.

Practice

Put your skills and knowledge into practice with the following question.

2 Write a narrative account analysing changes in the lives of cowboys in the years 1865–1874.

You may use the following in your answer:

- Abilene as the first cow town (1867).
- The introduction of barbed wire (1874).

You **must** also use information of your own.　　(8 marks)

....

....

....

....

....

....

....

....

....

....

....

....

....

....

....

....

....

....

....

....

....

....

....

....

It is a good idea to quickly plan your answer first by making a list of relevant key events in the period covered by the question. For example:

1865 = end of the Civil War

1867 = first cow town

1870 = John Iliff's ranch increased to 16 000 acres

1874 = barbed wire introduced

This gives you a structure for your answer.

Links You can revise changes in the lives of cowboys on page 18.

It is very important to bring information of your own into your answer. You must use your own information in order to make your answer as strong as possible.

Remember to analyse the links between the events and support this with relevant information. You can highlight that you are making connections with phrases such as: 'Because of this...'; 'As a result of..'; and 'This led to...'. Your analysis can look at causation, consequence and change.

Practice

Use this page to continue your answer to Question 2.

....

....

....

....

....

....

....

....

....

....

....

....

....

....

....

....

....

....

....

....

....

....

....

....

....

....

Remember, this is not a question about the growth of the cattle industry but about **changes in the lives of cowboys** as a result of changes in the cattle industry. For example, the long drives after the end of the Civil War meant that cowboys spent three months or longer herding cows from Texas up to Kansas. What was the impact of this on cowboys' lives?

Your answer should set out a clear sequence of events that leads to an outcome. In this case, the outcome is the move for many cowboys from life on the long trails to life on a ranch on the open range.

Make sure you only cover the range of years given in the question: 1865–74. This is not a question where you can use your knowledge of the winter of 1886–87.

Make sure you support your analysis with a good range of accurate and relevant detail throughout your answer.

Practice

Put your skills and knowledge into practice with the following question.

3 Explain **two** of the following:

☐ • The importance of the Homestead Act of 1862 for the settlement of the West.   **(8 marks)**

☐ • The importance of the 1849 Gold Rush for problems of lawlessness in early towns and settlements. **(8 marks)**

☐ • The importance of President Grant's 'Peace Policy' (1868) for changes in the way of life of the Plains Indians.   **(8 marks)**

(Total for Question 3 = 16 marks)

Although three events are listed, the question only asks you to pick **two** of them for your answer: you should pick the two you can answer best and write two separate answers.

Pay careful attention to what exactly you are being asked to explain: the second part of each event gives you the specific focus of the question.

Links You can revise the importance of the Homestead Act on page 13. For more about the 1849 Gold Rush, turn to pages 6 and 11. Find out more about President Grant's 'Peace Policy' on page 21.

If you decide to answer Question 3 (i), turn to page 44. If you decide to answer Question 3 (ii), turn to page 46. To answer Question 3 (iii), turn to page 48.

Write a sentence defining your event and then at least two paragraphs explaining its importance. Remember to include sufficient detail in your answer and try and link your consequences together.

Answering the question

On the exam paper you will see exam question 3 on one page and then you'll turn onto a new page to start your answer to your first choice of question.

In the exam you will have two full pages of paper for each of the two questions that you choose to do.

You should spend about 13 minutes answering each of the questions you have chosen.

Practice

Put your skills and knowledge into practice with the following question.

3 Indicate which part you are answering by marking a cross in the box ☒. If you change your mind, put a line through the box ☒ and then indicate your new answer with a cross ☒.

☒ The importance of the Homestead Act of 1862 for the settlement of the West

☐ The importance of the 1849 Gold Rush for problems of lawlessness in early towns and settlements.

☐ The importance of President Grant's 'Peace Policy' (1868) for changes in the way of life of the Plains Indians.

....
....
....
....
....
....
....
....
....
....
....
....
....
....
....
....
....
....
....
....

You can show which question you will answer first by putting a cross in the box next to that question. That saves a lot of time as you don't need to write the question out! If you put a cross next to the wrong question by mistake, don't worry. Just put a line through the cross and put a cross next to the question you have chosen to answer.

Question 3 is testing your ability to explain how and why an event is significant for a particular development. That means talking about consequences. For example, 'The Homestead Act was important for the settlement of the West because its offer of free land led to many migrants from Europe coming to settle on the Plains, such as the Mennonites.'

- Link to question
- Shows analysis
- Consequence
- AO1 information

A strong answer would explain two or three consequences of the event that show its importance and contain relevant factual knowledge. For example, six million acres had been homesteaded by 1876; nearly half all settled land in Nebraska being homestead lands.

Practice

Use this space to continue your answer to Question 3 (i) if necessary.

....
....
....
....
....
....
....
....
....
....
....
....
....
....
....
....
....
....
....
....
....
....
....
....
....
....
....
....

> Remember: you need to write about the importance of the Homestead Act of 1862 for the settlement of the West. Don't just describe what happened.

> You don't have to write a formal conclusion, but instead a single sentence summarising or briefly explaining your key points might help here. For example, you could say: 'The Homestead Act was important because the offer of virtually free land encouraged people from all over America and from Europe to settle in the West.'

> Make sure you support your explanation with a good range of accurate and relevant detail throughout your answer.

Practice

Put your skills and knowledge into practice with the following question.

3 Indicate which part you are answering by marking a cross in the box ☒. If you change your mind, put a line through the box ☒ and then indicate your new answer with a cross ☒.

☐ The importance of the Homestead Act of 1862 for the settlement of the West

☒ The importance of the 1849 Gold Rush for problems of lawlessness in early towns and settlements.

☐ The importance of President Grant's 'Peace Policy' (1868) for changes in the way of life of the Plains Indians.

....

....

....

....

....

....

....

....

....

....

....

....

....

....

....

....

....

....

....

....

....

When you start your second answer to Question 3, you again show which question you are answering by putting a cross next to that question. You don't have to answer the questions in the order in which they are presented.

Although there are equal marks for AO1 and AO2, if your answer doesn't do any AO2 analysis of consequence/ significance, it won't be able to get more than a maximum of 2 marks out of 8. So, remember to analyse importance!

Using words to indicate consequences and significance will help you keep your AO2 focus. For example: 'The Gold Rush intensified the...'.

Practice

Use this space to continue your answer to Question 3 (ii) if necessary.

....
....
....
....
....
....
....
....
....
....
....
....
....
....
....
....
....
....
....
....
....
....
....
....
....
....
....
....
....
....

The mark scheme for Question 3 says that the best answers:
- show analysis of importance (AO2)
- have a clear structure so it is easy to follow the analysis (AO2)
- include accurate and relevant information (AO1)
- show good knowledge and understanding of the period (AO1).

Remember to use your AO1 information to back up your analysis. For example, you could say: 'Before the California Gold Rush, around 5000 people had migrated west along the Oregon Trail. The Gold Rush led directly to an enormous increase in migrants: tens of thousands travelled west along the Oregon Trail in April 1849. Although some returned, many stayed in California, leading to a boom in the new state's economy based on mining, trading and farming.'

Had a go ☐   Nearly there ☐   Nailed it! ☐

Practice

Put your skills and knowledge into practice with the following question.

3 Indicate which part you are answering by marking a cross in the box ☒. If you change your mind, put a line through the box ☒ and then indicate your new answer with a cross ☒.

☐ The importance of the Homestead Act of 1862 for the settlement of the West

☐ The importance of the 1849 Gold Rush for problems of lawlessness in early towns and settlements.

☒ The importance of President Grant's 'Peace Policy' (1868) for changes in the way of life of the Plains Indians.

....

....

....

....

....

....

....

....

....

....

....

....

....

....

....

....

....

....

....

When you start your second answer to Question 3, you again show which question you are answering by putting a cross next to that question. You don't have to answer the questions in the order in which they are presented.

Although there are equal marks for AO1 and AO2, if your answer doesn't do any AO2 analysis of consequence/significance, it won't be able to get more than a maximum of 2 marks out of 8. So remember to analyse importance!

Using words to indicate consequences and significance will help you keep your AO2 focus. For example: 'The 'Peace Policy' brought about…'.

Remember: you are looking at how important the 'Peace Policy' was for the way of life of the Plains Indians. What changes did it introduce? Did these changes make life better or worse for the Plains Indians?

For each point you make, always then explain how it relates to the question.

Practice

Use this space to continue your answer to Question 3 (iii) if necessary.

....

....

....

....

....

....

....

....

....

....

....

....

....

....

....

....

....

....

....

....

....

....

....

....

....

....

The mark scheme for Question 3 says that the best answers:
- show analysis of importance (AO2)
- have a clear structure so it is easy to follow the analysis (AO2)
- include accurate and relevant information (AO1)
- show good knowledge and understanding of the period (AO1).

Your accurate and relevant information could include points such as:
- The 'Peace Policy' included a $2 million budget for improving reservations.

Remember to use your AO1 information to back up your analysis. For example, you could say: 'Before the Peace Policy, reservation agents were often corrupt, which made life very hard for Plains Indian tribes because they were cheated of provisions and sold low-quality food and clothing for very high prices. The Peace Policy aimed to change this and improve life on the reservations by replacing corrupt agents with Quakers – religious men with a strong reputation for honesty, fairness and peaceful compassion.'

Answers

Where an example answer is given, this is not necessarily the only correct response. In most cases there is a range of responses that can gain full marks.

SUBJECT CONTENT

The early settlement of the West, c1835–c1862

Plains Indians

1. Plains Indians: social and tribal structures

Bands were the units that tribes were made up of. While Indians lived in bands all the time, many tribes only came together at certain times of year. Both bands and tribes had chiefs and councils. Band chiefs made up the tribe's councils in most tribes.

2. Plains Indians: survival on the Plains

Your answers could include two from the following:

- Horses were essential for hunting buffalo as, when buffalo were startled (e.g. by hunters), they would run away too quickly for hunters on foot to keep up. Horses could keep up with stampeding buffalo, and could be trained to keep running alongside a buffalo while the rider used both hands to fire arrows into the buffalo's side.

- Horses were used for transport, they dragged the travois on which Indians transported their property, and Indians also of course rode them from place to place.

- Horses were essential for Indian raids and warfare because Indians often needed to get in and out of conflict situations rapidly. Indian bows were deadly at short range but, until they began to acquire modern rifles, they had no long-range weapons. So, Indians used their horses to race close to enemies, fight, and then race out again.

- Horses were so important to Plains Indians that they became the main measure of wealth and importance in Plains Indian society. The more horses a man had, the higher his status.

- Horses also had an important role in Indian leisure and entertainment, with young people racing each other and out-performing each other in daring horse-riding tricks and stunts.

3. Plains Indians: beliefs

It was important to minimise the number of warriors killed in conflicts between tribes because warriors were also often important hunters for the tribe or band, and if they were killed or badly wounded this would reduce the amount of food the band had to live on. Warriors were also in charge of deciding when buffalo hunts were to be held, and how the hunts were to be organised. Warriors were important because they formed the guard units that protected the bands from raids by other tribes, which would otherwise threaten to steal food, horses and people, and kill people.

4. US government policy and the Plains Indians

As well as keeping Indians and white settlers/migrants apart, the government hoped that reservations would encourage Plains Indians to learn farming, which would enable them to integrate better into white American ways of life. As long as Indians depended on hunting and gathering, the US government believed that they would never learn to respect property or learn to better themselves and become civilised. If Indians learned to farm, they would (the government believed) understand that their plot of farmland belonged to their family, not to the tribe as a whole or to the spirits of nature. Then they would want to learn ways of getting more out of their farmland so they could live more comfortable lives. They would become integrated into American society, buying tools and equipment to help them farm, and selling their farm products for money, then using the money to improve their homes and pay for education for their children.

Westward migration
5. Why move west?

The US government wanted people to migrate west to settle in Oregon and California and establish those areas as US territories. It encouraged migration west in the following ways:

- Between 1838 and 1842, the US government funded an expedition to explore Oregon, which led to a map of Oregon being published in 1841.

- In 1841, the US government provided $30 000 for an expedition to map the Oregon Trail and published reports that would help migrants to get to Oregon. John Fremont was the leader of the expedition and his published reports were very influential. They were the guidebook that migrants used on the Trail.

- Also, in 1841, the Pre-Emption Act allowed people who were squatting on US federal land (occupying it without having any legal right to do so) to buy 160 acres of the land at a cheap price.

- In 1846, the US government agreed a treaty with Great Britain that ended joint US-British ownership of Oregon territory and established the border of the USA and British territories in Canada.

- In 1850, the Donation Land Claim Act gave 320 acres of federal land in Oregon Territory to any white adult property-owning male who claimed it, plus another 320 acres if the man was married. The claimants then had to work the land for 4 years in order to get full ownership.

6. The Gold Rush of 1849

These answers are for each of the three 'importance of…' statements given in the question.

The Gold Rush of 1849 was important for settlement of the West because it was a major pull factor for migrants to move west from the eastern USA, and also for people to come to the West from all over the world. Although, many of these were single men who planned to get rich and then go home again, because most failed to find gold, a large number stayed to either keep searching for gold in the mountains, or moved into other occupations, such as farming or working in trades that supplied prospectors and miners. As a result, California's population boomed (from around 8 000 people, excluding Indians, in 1846 to over 300 000, by 1854) and it became a state in 1850. The success of California was a pull factor for more people to come west from the eastern USA, mostly along the Oregon and California Trails.

The Gold Rush was important for relations between white Americans and native Americans for two main reasons. Firstly, the new migrants led to the virtual extinction of the native Californian Indian population, not only because of the diseases they carried with them, to which the Indians had no natural resistance, but also because the new migrants murdered Indians and forced Indians away from any land they wanted to use for themselves. Bounties were paid for dead Indians and white settlers carried out massacres of Indians, often in the misplaced fear that the Indians were in some way a threat to white settlers. Some historians say that what happened to the Californian Indians was genocide. For the Plains Indians, the enormous increase in the numbers travelling through their lands along the Oregon Trail led to tensions. The main cause of such tension was that the white migrants disturbed buffalo and the oxen teams that pulled their wagons (often four oxen per wagon) and the cattle that the migrants brought with them ate the grass along the trail, which made these areas useless for hunting. Tribes kept watch over the migrants, therefore, to make sure they did not start to cause this destruction further into Indian lands. The migrants worried that the Indians they saw were planning to attack them, and demanded Army protection, with forts along the Trail. This demand led to the Fort Laramie Treaty of 1851.

The Gold Rush was important for increases in lawlessness in the West because the huge population increases meant existing arrangements for justice and law enforcement were completely swamped. The population of San Francisco increased from just 500 people in 1847, to 25 000 by 1849 – far beyond what local law enforcement could deal with. Gangs took over the city and criminals were, for a time, able to do whatever they wanted, without fear of punishment. This led to the formation of the first vigilance committee in San Francisco in 1851. Continued immigration to the city led to tensions because of racism: especially crimes against Chinese immigrants. Racism by law enforcement in California meant that crimes against Chinese people were often ignored. In the mining camps, miners formed their own courts to deal with petty crimes, and to settle disputes over claims. More serious crimes were a huge problem too, with robbers and swindlers hoping to take advantage of those lucky miners and prospectors who found gold. Vigilance committees spread to the mining camps, too, because there was no other way for the miners and prospectors to protect themselves.

7. The Oregon Trail and the Donner Party

This is a sample answer: note how it makes links to provide analysis and narrative:

When the Donner Party migrants reached Fort Bridger in the Rocky Mountains in July 1846, the group split. Around 80 migrants, including both Donner brothers, decided to try a new short cut that left the Oregon Trail and cut some 550 km off the established route. The reason they did this was because a trail guide, called Lansford Hastings, had written about this short cut in a pamphlet and described it as a fine road with plenty of grass and water. However, believing Hastings' account was the first big mistake of the Donner Party, because Hastings had in fact not used the short cut himself – he simply thought it should work.

The short cut actually caused long delays and meant the group that followed it began to fight amongst themselves. Unlike the well-established Oregon Trail, where migrants could just follow the ruts left by the wagon wheels of previous travellers, this route had not been marked out and was hard to follow. While the Oregon Trail had been cleared for wagons, here the terrain was rugged and rocky, with steep slopes and deep canyons. The wagons had to go very slowly to avoid accidents. The party had to try out different spots to cross rivers before they found the safest points to cross – unlike the Oregon Trail where river ferries waited to transfer migrants across (for a fee). There were also stretches of desert with no water or grass for the livestock – along the Oregon Trail there were forts where migrants could take on new provisions and places where livestock could find pasture, but there was none of that organisation here. By the time the Donner Party reached the foothills of the Sierra Nevada Mountains, it was mid-October. The processes set up for the Oregon Trail were designed to get migrants through the mountains before winter – the Donner Party had failed to make this essential deadline.

At a result, by the start of November, the wagons were high up in the mountains, but before they could make it over the pass, snowstorms trapped the Donner Party. Their livestock died and soon their food ran out. The first migrant died of starvation on 15 December. When rescuers from California reached the party in February, only half of the original 80 were alive – and most of those had only survived by eating those who had died. The Donner Party had left the relative security of the Oregon Trail without having properly prepared themselves for the problems of finding a new way to California.

8. The Mormon migration

One possible answer (but not the only one!) could look like this (numbers and bold text have been added to help show the key events and connections):

In 1845, the Mormons were forced to leave Illinois after riots against them, which killed their leader, Joseph Smith.

As a result of this, the Mormons had a new leader, Brigham Young, who believed God had told him to lead the Mormons to Salt Lake Valley.

2 In June 1846, Mormons congregated at Omaha, at the start of the Oregon Trail.

Because June was too late in the year for migration, **this led to** Young deciding that the Mormons must stay in Omaha through the winter, which involved enduring much hardship and suffering.

3 In April 1847, Brigham Young and his small advance party set out on the 2000 km journey to Salt Lake Valley.

As a result of Young's careful organisation, the advance party had no problems finding the route from the Oregon Trail to Salt Lake Valley.

4 Young reached Salt Lake Valley in July 1847, and recognised it as the place God wanted the Mormons to settle.

Because Salt Lake Valley was outside the USA at this time, this meant that the Mormons felt they would be safe from persecution here.

5 In August 1847, a second, much larger group of 1500 Mormons arrived at Salt Lake Valley.

As a result of Young's advance party marking out the route, clearing the way for wagons and finding good sources of water and pasture, and good places to rest along the route, the second group had far fewer challenges making the migration than would otherwise have been the case.

6 The Mormons sent parties of settlers out to set up new settlements over a wide area.

One consequence of this was that the new settlements specialised in particular resources or products, such as providing timber, water, minerals or particular food crops, which were then brought back to the Salt Lake Valley to help the settlers there deal with its harsh environment.

9. Problems of farming the Plains

The lack of timber on the Plains meant that settlers had nothing else to build houses with. However, sod houses did have some advantages: the sods were free and farmers needed to cut them out of the soil anyway in order to be able to plough the earth underneath; the earth was fireproof, which was important given prairie fires, and the thick earth walls also provided good insulation against summer heat and winter cold.

Conflict and tension

10. The Fort Laramie Treaty, 1851

Your two consequences of the Fort Laramie Treaty of 1851 could include:

• The Fort Laramie Treaty increased white settlement in the West because it arranged for safe passage of white settlers along the Oregon Trail.

• The Fort Laramie Treaty punctured the concept of

a permanent Indian frontier between the eastern states of the USA and the Plains Indians by allowing white migrants to cross Plains Indian lands along the Oregon Trail.

• The Fort Laramie Treaty saw the Plains Indian tribes involved (including the Arapaho, Blackfoot, Cheyenne, Crow, Dakota Sioux, Lakota Sioux, and Mandan nations) agreeing to let railroad surveyors enter their lands in safety, which was an important step towards transcontinental railroads.

• The Fort Laramie Treaty saw the US government prioritise the needs of white settlers over the previous commitments it had made about Indian lands in the Indian Trade and Intercourse Act of 1834. This process would continue, so that each time there was conflict over resources between settlers and Indians, the Indians were usually, in the end, the ones who gave up their lands.

• Although the Fort Laramie Treaty did not establish reservations for the Plains Indians, reservations were a consequence of the Treaty because of the way the 1851 Treaty set out which tribe held which lands, and mapped this.

• The Fort Laramie Treaty saw the Plains Indians tribes involved agreeing to the terms of the Treaty in return for an annuity (yearly payment) of $50 000, as long as they kept to the Treaty terms. This annuity became a lever for the government to use against the Indians and had the consequence of starting to encourage dependence of some Plains Indians on the government for food.

11. Lawlessness!

Two ways in which local communities tried to tackle lawlessness could include:

• Miners' courts: this was a way that mining and prospecting communities tried to deal with the lack of a justice system in the isolated mountain locations, in which camps of thousands of men suddenly sprang up following the discovery of gold. Miners' courts not only gave out judgements to settle disputed claims between prospectors and miners, they were also involved in developing new laws about mining and prospecting claims, and adapting laws from when California was Mexican; these laws were eventually made part of Californian state law, which had not been able to keep up with the rapid changes.

• Vigilantes: when there was no law enforcement to control crime, or when law enforcement was inadequate or corrupted by the criminals, local citizens could form vigilance committees. Often, the members of the committees remained anonymous to protect them from reprisals. The vigilantes would capture suspected criminals, try them and sentence them; those that were sentenced to death would be lynched. A death sentence was not inevitable – the San Francisco vigilance committees of 1851 judged half their suspects to be not guilty, and of those judged guilty they handed half over to the police.

• Lynch mobs – when local communities thought that

wanted criminals, who had been arrested by local law officers, might escape justice (for example, that they might be rescued from jail by other members of their gang, or be judged not guilty), a mob would arrive at the town jail, demand the suspects be handed over by the law officers, and lynch them.

- Towns and districts could elect sheriffs and marshals, once the territory they lived in had over 5 000 inhabitants.

12. Sheriffs and marshals

Two ways the federal government tried to bring law and order to the West could include:

- It appointed US marshals and deputy marshals, who were responsible for law and order in territories and towns.

- It appointed judges to tour the West and try criminals in federal courts.

- It helped to bring the railroads and electric telegraph communications to the West, which meant it was easier for law enforcers to reach the towns or get news of trouble and coordinate a response.

- It encouraged migration to the West. Increased population meant the territories could become states that could employ their own law enforcement officers. More families settled in the West who wanted to live in safe towns where the law was enforced.

Development of the Plains, c1862–c1876

Settlement in the West

13. The Homestead Act, 1862

Ways in which the Civil War was important in the settlement of the West could include:

1 The Homestead Act: the southern states had opposed reforms similar to the Homestead Act before the Civil War. They did not want the main model for settling the West to be individual family farms, in case this prevented the development of large farms worked by slaves, which was the basis of the economy in many southern states. When the southern states temporarily left the USA to form their Confederacy in 1861, there was no longer enough opposition in Congress to block the Homestead Act being passed. The Homestead Act went on to have significant impacts on the settlement of the West.

2 The Pacific Railroad Act: the southern states had recognised that the proposed routes of the First Transcontinental Railroad were designed to favour the industrial cities of the North and risked isolating the southern states, so they had blocked the passing of acts to subsidise the railroad. As with the Homestead Act, when the southern states were no longer in Congress, this enabled the northern states to pass the Pacific Railroad Act (1862). This enabled the First Transcontinental Railroad to get underway, and an important part of the way the railroad

companies were funded was through government grants of land to them to sell to settlers. Railroads across the West had a very significant impact on settlement of the West: as a route for migrants, as a way of settlers selling farming products and buying industrial products, as a focus for the cattle industry and for the formation of towns and cities and the selling of land for settlers.

3 Impact on the South: the eventual defeat of the Confederate states in the Civil War and the abolition of slavery caused a deep depression in the economy of the South of the USA. This had an impact on a new wave of settlers looking for a new start in life, including freed slaves and former soldiers.

14. The First Transcontinental Railroad, 1869

Your impacts could include three of the following:

- On the cattle industry: the railroad railheads were used to transport cattle to the cities of the East for processing, which boosted the development of Plains cow towns and the development of ranching on the Plains.

- On settler farming: the railroads brought in settlers and linked up settler farms with the industrial centres of the east. Trains carried farm produce to the cities and brought agricultural machinery and other industrial products to the West, enabling farming to develop and settlers to deal better with the challenges of farming the Plains.

- On law and order: faster communication between settlements enabled law officers to get out to trouble spots quicker, as did the electric telegraph which ran alongside the railroad tracks.

- On crime and lawlessness: trains carried gold and money between west and east and were targeted by train robbers. The work gangs that built the railroads were largely Chinese and African American, and these people were the focus of criminal acts, due to racism.

- On settlement of the Plains: railroad companies sold land to settlers and areas closest to the railroad sold fastest and for the highest prices, because of its benefits to settlers (communication with eastern states and markets).

- On migration to the West: from 1869, the numbers using the Oregon Trail and other trails dropped as people took the train instead.

- On the Plains Indians: railroads disrupted buffalo migrations (especially when fenced in by barbed wire), railroads brought the hunters that exterminated the buffalo herds and railroads transported the buffalo hides and bones back to the industrial cities for processing. Trains sparked fires that burnt grass, depriving the buffalo and Indian horses of pasture, and trains brought settlers, who forced the Indians off their land. Surveying and construction of the railroads led to conflict between Indians and construction teams. Indians were persuaded to give up their lands along railroad routes and move to reservations away from the area instead.

15. Homesteaders: finding solutions

There were five main ways in which the Timber Culture Act aimed to reduce the high rate of failure for people trying to get started farming the Plains.

- 160 acres was not enough land in drier parts of the Plains: adding another 160 acres of land meant a better chance of producing enough crops or livestock products to make a living.

- Tying this grant of an additional 160 acres to planting trees on half the new land aimed to increase the amount of timber available on the Plains for fencing and construction.

- Trees would also act as windbreaks, providing some shelter for crops from the strong prairie winds.

- It was believed that planting trees would encourage more rain (Americans believed the same thing about ploughing the land – 'rain follows the plough'), though this is not something that is believed today.

- Trees would provide settlers with fuel for cooking and heating. Many settlers had to rely on burning grass or buffalo 'chips' (buffalo dung).

16. More problems for law and order

1 If rail companies and stagecoach companies and other rich business people employed Pinkerton detectives to protect their property and employees, this suggests that it was because they could not rely on police forces, sheriffs and marshals and their deputies to do this policing job for them. This would fit in with the concept of the West as being lawless because of a lack of law officers to enforce the law.

Pinkertons might also be used in cases where companies suspected that local law officers were corrupt: either that they were being paid or intimidated by gangs not to act against them, or were actually in on the crimes themselves and were getting a share of what got stolen. Because Pinkertons was a private company and not part of local communities, it was not so open to corruption.

Local sheriffs and town marshals had no training in detective work – few police forces had any detectives in this period – so the Pinkertons provided these skills, allowing local law enforcement to stick to their main role of keeping the peace.

2 The main impact came from reducing the problems of communicating across the huge areas covered by law officers in the West. Because electric telegraphs were constructed along the railroad routes, law officers had an improved ability to communicate with each other and coordinate their efforts in controlling crime, and in responding to reports of

trouble. Railroads offered a safer way of transporting suspects from local jails, which were not often very secure, to proper jails in bigger towns, where they could wait for their trials (which could be properly organised in bigger towns with experienced judges and lawyers) and be tried by juries who were not from the local area where the crime had been committed, making them less biased and also less likely to have been intimidated or corrupted by friends of the accused.

The cattle industry
17. Cattle trails and cow towns

While farming on the Plains developed as thousands of individual homestead families ploughed and cultivated the land, cattle ranching was dominated by a few very rich cattle barons who controlled enormous ranches and hundreds of thousands of cattle. This was partly the result of the role of investors – the cattle industry in the 1870s was seen as a certain way of making money because of the combination of free grazing land and cheap cows on the one hand, and rocketing demand for beef in the growing industrial cities of the USA and elsewhere (once beef could be refrigerated while it was being transported, keeping it fresh) on the other. Investors preferred large scale operations: it was difficult to invest in lots of small ranches and large scale operations had economies of scale that made them more profitable – they could get good deals from the railroad companies for transportation, for example. Backed by all this investment, the cattle barons could afford to build up even bigger herds, over even larger areas of the Plains. Because they were so rich, cattle barons became very important men in their states and territories, especially in places such as Wyoming, that did not have much of anything else happening. This allowed the cattle barons to block the development of other economic activities, like homesteading, that might have threatened ranching and to influence government in issues such as who should supply food to army forts and the Indian reservations that were under the control of the federal government.

18. Changing roles for cowboys

Reasons include:

- The cattle industry itself changed: driving cattle huge distances to railheads and cow towns was dangerous because of the weather, stampeding cattle, wild animals, hostile Indians, cattle rustlers, and the risk of drowning in rivers or quicksand, etc. Long drives up from Texas continued, but more and more cattle began to be raised on ranches on the Plains. Drives still took place from the ranches to the railheads, but these were much shorter: days or a week, rather than weeks or months.

- Round-ups were still an important part of open range ranching: the cattle were allowed to wander freely and were then rounded up in spring, along with their new calves that needed to be sorted out and branded for the ranch their mother belonged to.

One change for cowboys on the Plains was the winter weather: cattle would need rescuing from snow drifts, would need help breaking through the snow to find grass, or would wander long distances away from the ranch as they turned away from the winter winds and kept walking until they found some shelter.

- As farming began to develop over the Plains, however, some open-range ranches came under pressure to fence in their animals to stop them wandering onto farmers' crops or getting mixed up with the farmers' own livestock. Having cattle fenced in on the ranch rather than roaming free changed cowboys' roles significantly, because now they were employed much more in ensuring the cattle had enough to eat – so cowboys might be responsible for cutting and carting hay around the ranch – and making sure fences were put up and maintained.

- By the 1890s, after the bust, ranches became more specialized, with smaller herds of better quality, purer breeds of cattle. The work of looking after these cows became more specialized, also, with more attention given to what the cows were eating and when, different treatments to get rid of pests and parasites, and specialised breeding programmes.

19. Ranchers vs homesteaders

Ranching needed enormous areas of land to be profitable: large herds of cattle needed to be able to roam over big areas of Plains grassland to find enough food to eat. Very few ranchers could afford to buy all that land, but the point about the development of the cattle industry on the Plains was that no money was needed: public, federal land – land that hadn't been claimed or wasn't Indian land – was free to use for grazing animals. That was one reason why the cattle industry was so profitable. However, the Homestead Act gave 160-acre plots of public land to anyone with $10 to file a claim, and that public land became their private property if they proved up (the process of meeting the requirements to become the legal owner of the land: building a home, farming the land and paying a $6 fee). This was a major problem for ranchers in areas of the Plains that were suitable for farming, because homesteaders were most likely to file claims to land with water sources, and to the best land that was also the best grazing land. Cattle ranchers needed water for their cattle, and if a homesteader filed a claim that included the only spring or pond for miles around, and then fenced in their claim, then the rancher would have lost access to water and to the best grazing land. From the farmer's point of view, open range ranching was not compatible with farming for two main reasons. The first was that cattle would eat their crops, often breaking down weaker fencing to get to it (before barbed wire was in common use), and ranch cattle would get mixed up with the farmer's own cattle. Secondly, the mixing of cattle could spread diseases, but it also caused problems when farmers' cattle got rounded up with ranch cattle, or ranch cattle got rounded up with farmers' cattle. Ranchers would often accuse farmers of rustling their cattle (stealing it), especially with regard to calves born on the open range before the spring round up that had not been branded with a mark identifying them as a particular ranch's property.

Changes for Plains Indians
20. Impacts on the Plains Indians

Your answer may include the following points:

- The discovery of gold in California in 1848 led to an enormous movement of prospectors from the east of the USA (and from all over the world) to California: 200 000 of them travelled along the Oregon Trail. This had a major impact on the resources of Plains Indians, who had lands along the Oregon Trail, increasing tension between whites and Indians. This was land that had been promised to the Indians, and which was supposed to be protected from whites behind a permanent Indian frontier. The whites called for army protection against Indian attacks, and this led directly to the Fort Laramie Treaty in which the Indians agreed to allow whites to cross their lands in return for annuity payments.

- The discovery of gold in 1859 in the Rocky Mountains led to prospectors trespassing on Cheyenne and Arapaho lands, breaking the Fort Laramie Treaty. Again, the whites demanded protection from Indians and the result was the Fort Wise Treaty of 1861, which moved Cheyenne and Arapaho tribes to smaller reservations away from the lands the whites wanted to use. Not all the Indians agreed to the Treaty, however, leading to war with the US Army. This conflict led to the Sand Creek Massacre.

- When gold was discovered in Montana, in 1863, prospectors from the East used a new trail, named the Bozeman Trail, as the quickest way across the Plains to the gold fields. This trail went across the hunting lands of the Lakota Sioux, breaking the Fort Laramie Treaty. Again, the white settlers demanded forts and US Army protection from Indian attack. The US government sent negotiators to agree a new treaty allowing safe passage along the Bozeman Trail, but at the same time the US Army began building forts, incensing chief Red Cloud and leading to Red Cloud's War. To end the conflict, the US government agreed the Fort Laramie Treaty (1868).

21. Impacts of government policy

Your answer could include the following points:

- The traditional way of life for Plains Indians was based on hunting, especially buffalo hunting but also hunting other animals, such as deer. Although some reservations included hunting grounds, as time went on the size of reservations decreased and it became harder and harder for Indians to find enough food for the whole tribe through hunting without leaving the reservation.

- Buffalo migrations were not predictable – the herds roamed fairly randomly over the Plains – and the traditional way of life for many Plains Indian tribes was to follow the herds through the summer, living a nomadic lifestyle. Reservation life was completely different: instead of moving from place to place, most Indians remained in one place.

- In return for moving to reservations, tribes were promised annuities – annual payments in return for the land they had given up. These annuities were frequently paid in food, or partly in food, partly in other goods and partly in money. As it became harder to find enough food, tribes became more and more dependent on these government deliveries of food. This did not reflect the traditional ways of life of the Indians.

- Reservations were designed to encourage Indians to give up traditional ways of life and learn about farming and Christianity, so that Indians could start to integrate into white American ways of life. Certain practices, such as sending Indian children to schools away from the reservation, meant that children did not learn the traditions of their tribe. This had negative consequences for the future of the tribe and its traditional customs and practices.

22. The Indian Wars

Your answer may include the following points:

In Little Crow's War (1862), problems with the reservation system were central to the tensions that led to open conflict.

- The Dakota Sioux had agreed to move to two small reservations, in 1851, in return for large annuity payments ($80 000).

- However, before the annuity payments could be released, local traders demanded that the Indians pay back debts of $200 000 that the traders claimed they were owed.

- The reservations were too small for the Indians to support themselves by hunting, so they left the reservation to hunt, causing conflict and the punishment of having government food supplies reduced.

- Over the years, the reservation agents and the local traders cheated the Indians shamelessly. For example, they would hold back annuity payments until the Indians were starving, and then charge very high prices for low quality food.

- Whites began to settle on portions of good farming land on the reservation and, despite the Indians' complaints, nothing was done to stop this.

- In 1858, the continued allegations about debts from the traders meant the Indians had half the reservation land taken away from them, despite being promised it was theirs forever.

- By 1862, the Indians were starving following crop failures. The reservation agents did nothing to help.

These tensions were all involved in the conflict in 1862, which began when Indians raided the agency storehouses on the reservation and distributed the food stored there to their starving families.

Reservation problems were also important in the conflict that involved Black Kettle and the Sand Creek Massacre.

- The Fort Wise Treaty of 1861 saw Arapaho and Cheyenne chiefs agreeing to the tribes being moved to a reservation in east Colorado, away from the areas needed by whites.

- However, although some Indians moved to the reservations, large numbers of Dog Soldiers, young warrior brotherhoods, did not want to live on a reservation, refused to move and continued to attack and harass prospectors crossing Colorado Territory.

- Colonel Chivington's 1864 massacre of more than 150 Indians, mostly women and children, was a response to this conflict. Hearing of it, the Dog Soldiers were convinced they had been right not to agree to the Fort Wise Treaty and that the US government was not to be trusted. They attacked army forts and killed many white settlers.

- In 1864. the US government could not spare troops from the Civil War to fight against the Cheyenne and Arapaho, so a new treaty was agreed in 1865, involving a much bigger new reservation and continued hunting rights on the tribes' traditional hunting lands in Colorado Territory. However, once the Civil War was won, the government went back on this deal.

Conflicts and conquest, c1876–c1895
Changing times
23. Changes in farming

Ways could include:

- One problem of farming the Plains was isolation: homesteaders were cut off. The spread of railroads enabled homesteaders to keep in touch better with family and communities, because railroads speeded up the postal system and made it possible to travel cheaply.

- The spread of the railroad network across the West made it easier for farmers to export crops to markets in the East and abroad. This brought more money into farming, helping its development.

- The railroad linked farmers in the West with the industrial cities. This allowed manufacturers to respond to farmers' needs by developing improved ploughs to plough up the tough prairie sod; ploughs that ploughed deeper for dry farming methods; seed drills that planted seeds deeper in the soil, important for dry farming; improved windmills and pumps to solve the problems of water shortage; and barbed wire. None of these new developments would have become widespread without a cheap and efficient way to get them out to farmers in the West.

- The link provided by the railroad also enabled farmers in the West to buy things to improve their quality of life: household products, new houses (made of timber and tar paper) to replace their sod houses, new clothes and entertainment products, such as pianos, books and magazines. These made life more bearable and reduced the number of homesteaders giving up.

24. Changes in the cattle industry

- Smaller ranches meant cattle were not as far away from the ranch, making it easier to rescue them from trouble.
- Smaller herds meant fewer animals to rescue from the open range.
- Smaller herds might not have overgrazed the open range covered by the ranch as badly as some of the biggest herds.
- When drought and lack of pasture began to affect herds in the summer of 1886, smaller ranches had less of a challenge to supplement their food and find water sources.

25. Continued settlement growth

The main differences in the migrations were:

- The Mormons had chosen to follow a particular religion that was discriminated against by other white Americans; black Americans faced persecution and discrimination in every aspect of their lives and had no choice about it.
- The Mormons were an organised group with a common set of beliefs and purpose; the Exodusters were not an organised movement; the name Exodusters was used to describe a migration that people were making for lots of different reasons.
- While the Mormons had a leader, there was no leader for the Exoduster migration. Brigham Young was also a particularly strong and dedicated leader, whose idea it was to migrate to Salt Lake Valley.
- The Mormon migration was very well funded: it had lots of money raised by Mormons across America, who continued to send money to the migrants year after year. This helped the Mormons survive in Salt Lake Valley. The Exodusters were not funded at all. This meant they had to rely on support from the state they had migrated to, and this did not help them much.
- The Mormon migration was very well planned, with the route surveyed in advance: a great deal of research was done on how best to survive in Salt Lake Valley, and a clear idea formed of how the new settlements would work and support each other. The Exodusters did not have this plan: these were desperate people who hoped that God would help them and that the people who had fought against slavery in the Civil War would welcome them and help ex-slaves make a new life.
- The Mormons were moving to a largely unpopulated region that was, at the time, outside the US government system, while the Exodusters were moving to states where the best land had already been taken by white settlers and there was already an established state political system that was dominated by whites and served white interests.

- Many of the Exodusters passed through regions with yellow fever and caught the disease, meaning that when they arrived in Kansas they were very ill. Although many Mormons had suffered from their winters in Omaha, they did not have this same problem in their migrations to the Salt Lake Valley.
- Many of the Exodusters moved to towns and got jobs working for whites; it was not primarily a migration to start new settlements (although some all-black towns and cities, e.g. Nicodemus, were established).
- The initial Mormon migration was followed by many more over the years, reinforcing the settlements they were building, whereas the problems and disappointments of the 1879 Exodusters meant that very few migrants from the South continued to move to Kansas from 1880, and some of those that did migrate to the West in 1879 tended to keep on moving to other states looking for a better situation.

Continuing conflict
26. Billy the Kid and Wyatt Earp

Arguments for lawlessness increasing could include:

- The increased tensions over land use, especially between big cattle ranchers and homesteaders/ smaller ranchers, led to increased lawlessness as the warring parties bought in armed support – gunfighters such as Billy the Kid or the Earp brothers.
- Corruption and intimidation of law officers was a reason why lawlessness did not always decrease – the Earp brothers are an example of this.
- The West remained a place where men were expected to solve their problems by themselves, rather than look to the government for support; this helps explain why feuds between families or groups led to increased violence until the situation got so bad that law enforcement from outside the region had to be called in, as was the case with Billy the Kid and Pat Garrett.

Arguments against increasing lawlessness could be:

- In most parts of the West, state law enforcement improved so that towns had well established police forces and impartial law courts. Most town governments voted for strict bans on carrying guns in towns, raised funds for town jails and expected their sheriffs, marshals and deputies to keep the peace. Federal control also increased in territories as the railroad network expanded over the West, as did the electric telegraph, making federal responses to trouble much faster. Certain places, such as Tombstone, were the exception.
- Even in towns like Tombstone, most citizens were not involved in lawlessness and wanted law and order. Although the Earps are usually portrayed as the heroes in films about the gunfight at the OK Corral, at the time, citizens of Tombstone were very critical of the Earps' actions, and were very much

opposed to Wyatt taking the law into his own hands and murdering the men he suspected of killing his brother, rather than doing his duty as an officer of the law.

- Where local situations had got out of hand, as they did in Lincoln County, federal or state governments did eventually implement measures to crack down on the problem. In the case of Billy the Kid, this had to wait for a new governor of New Mexico to be appointed, but the end result was a reduction in lawlessness, not an increase.

27. The Johnson County War

Your answer may make some or all of the following points:

It was significant that the 'invaders' were arrested because, usually, vigilantes acted for the community against threats to the community from lawlessness, which meant that vigilantes were protected by their community and were not arrested. It is also significant that these vigilantes were paid by the rich cattle owners of Wyoming, who had a lot of political power in the state government and the federal government. What was different in this case was that, in Johnson County, the community was against big ranchers and the WSGA (Wyoming Stock Growers Association). Juries in Johnson County did not convict suspected cattle rustlers because they believed they were homesteaders, not thieves, and small ranchers that the big cattle ranchers wanted to clear off 'their' land. That community had elected a sheriff sympathetic to their feelings, which is why the vigilantes came to be arrested.

It is significant that the 'invaders' were freed because the political power of the WSGA at state level, and the money that the WSGA had available, meant that they could ensure 'justice' went their way. Although the Johnson County community was opposed to the WSGA, state government and residents of the state capital, Cheyenne, were not: they considered the WSGA to be respectable businessmen trying to deal with criminals in a county that did not respect the law or the rights of respectable businessmen.

28. The Battle of the Little Big Horn, 1876

(a) The consequence of the Battle of the Little Big Horn for reservations was a determination by the US government and Army that Indians must be kept on their reservations. As a result of the defeat, Army divisions pursued the Sioux and Cheyenne tribes relentlessly so that, by 1876, most Indians had been forced back to their reservations, exhausted and short of food. Within five years, almost all the Sioux and Cheyenne were confined to their reservations, completely dependent on the US government for food and shelter.

(b) The consequence of the battle for previous treaties over land with the Indians was that the US government decided they could now be ignored:

when Indians had engaged in armed resistance with the US, they forfeited the right to have treaty deals. This meant the US government felt it could decide that Indians should be moved onto smaller reservations in worse conditions than before. The Sioux were told that if they didn't hand over control of the Black Hills, the US government would stop sending them food. Faced with starvation, the Sioux gave up the Black Hills, the Powder River Country and the Big Horn mountains, even though these were protected by treaties.

(c) Continued resistance by the Sioux became very difficult. The US Army significantly increased its troop numbers in the northern Plains and built new forts. The Sioux's weapons and horses were taken from them and they had to live under military rule. US Army divisions swept the Plains looking for off-reservation bands. In the spring of 1877, Crazy Horse surrendered to the US Army in Nebraska. When he was killed in the autumn, while under arrest at Fort Robinson, all effective resistance to the loss of their land by the Plains Indians was over. The Wounded Knee Massacre was portrayed at the time as being caused by Indian resistance, but it was not.

29. The Wounded Knee Massacre, 1890

Your answer is likely to conclude:

- The Ghost Dance alarmed the US Army and other whites, who thought it might be the start of a new outbreak of resistance from the Plains Indians.

- The Ghost Dance contributed directly to the massacre, in that the massacre began after Indians from Big Foot's band began dancing, which the US soldiers took as a sign of resistance.

- The Ghost Dance symbolised the Indians' dream of the white Americans leaving and everything becoming as it was in the past. It was frustrating for white Americans, who wanted the Indians to stop causing problems and accept they had lost. This frustration may have contributed to the massacre.

A way of life ends
30. Buffalo: hunting and extermination

Ways could include:

- hunting for sport (US Army soldiers were keen on this)
- hunting to make way for railroads
- hunting to feed railroad workers
- hunting to sell buffalo hides to make goods
- destroying their habitat by building on the land
- bringing cattle onto the Plains, which brought diseases that killed buffalo
- cattle and horses competed with the buffalo for grass.

31. Life on the reservations

Your two reasons could include:

- Reservations were often not large enough to support sufficient animals to feed the tribe through hunting, which meant Indians needed to rely on the government for food, and also meant they did not have the animal hides formerly used for clothing.

- Reservation lands were on the least fertile land, which made farming very difficult and crop failures very common, especially when there were droughts or grasshopper plagues. These meant less food was produced.

- Indian agents stole and cheated the reservation Indians out of food, and provided them with low quality food, all of which left the Indians without enough food to eat.

- The federal government used its rationing of food to the Indians as a way of controlling their behaviour. If there was any disobedience to the rules (for example, leaving the reservation to hunt), then food rations might be cut or the size of reservations reduced. The government exploited the dependence of the Indians and tried to make them even more dependent in order that they were more controllable.

- White settlers put pressure on the government to reduce the size of Indian reservations and open reservation land up for settlement. Settlers would illegally encroach on reservation land if there were fertile areas that they could take. All this meant less land to hunt on or grow food on.

- Reservations were often deeply depressing places, on poor land with no freedom, far from the sacred places of the tribe and places where their ancestors had been buried. Reservation Indians often lived surrounded by misery and illness. There did not seem to be much point for some Indians in struggling to get food or make clothing for themselves under such circumstances.

- Sending Indian children off-reservation to be educated in white culture meant these children came back to the reservation without all the traditional skills for hunting or finding food, or making their own clothes from natural resources.

- Once Indians were not allowed to have horses or weapons on reservations, they lost the key tools necessary to survive on the Plains. Indians who were proud of their heritage as hunters refused to learn farming, as this was associated with tribes that they did not consider worthy.

32. Changing government attitudes

Many whites believed that Indians should stop living as part of a communal tribal society, sharing many things in common, and start living as individuals or family units, like white Americans did. They believed that, while Indians shared things in common, they would never learn to improve their way of living because people who shared things in common never did – what was the point of spending time and effort improving

something if everyone else got to benefit from it for free? It did not occur to whites that the Indians had developed a way of living on the Plains sustainably, rather than overstocking it with cattle (which led to a collapse in the winter of 1886–87) or removing the grass from the soil and over-cultivating it with wheat through the dry farming system.

White views about assimilation also criticised tribal chiefs. White people thought that chiefs would only have power while the tribal system continued, so they were an obstacle to individualism being developed and assimilation taking place. Chiefs got their prestige because of their experience of the traditional ways of doing things, which meant they were not interested in innovation or improvement, as the whites thought. And chiefs, it was believed, could lead resistance, which would be very damaging to any progress made by the Indians towards 'civilisation'. Whites wanted Indians to assimilate so that they would respect and follow the leaders of white America, and give up their traditional ways of life and take up white customs and beliefs. This would stop Indian resistance to white control of all the land and resources in the USA.

PRACTICE
40. Practice

1 There are 4 marks available for each consequence. The two consequences are each marked separately. If your answer doesn't include any analysis of why it is a consequence, then the most you can get for your answer is 2 marks.

Your consequences could include two of the following:

- The second Fort Laramie Treaty (1868): in this treaty, the US government agreed to Red Cloud's demands to remove three forts and close the Bozeman Trail – a direct result of Red Cloud's victory.

- The closure of the Bozeman Trail: this could be a separate consequence on its own (but not a second one to the Fort Laramie Treaty, because it covers the same point).

- The US government recognised the land included in the Great Sioux Reservation as Indian territory, which whites were not allowed to settle on or pass through without Indian permission.

- Red Cloud agreed to move with his followers to a reservation: the Great Sioux reservation.

- Some chiefs, such as Sitting Bull and Crazy Horse, did not agree with the deal Red Cloud made and refused to sign the Fort Laramie Treaty. This had further consequences for conflict between Plains Indians and the US Army.

41. Practice

2 There are 8 marks on offer for this question: 4 marks for AO1 (knowledge and understanding) and 4 marks for AO2 (the analysis of consequence/ cause/change). A level 1 answer would get 1 or 2

marks only because the answer would only have very limited analysis and only very limited knowledge and understanding of the events and would be poorly organised. A level 3 answer (6-8 marks) would be very well structured so there is a clear sequence of events that leads to an outcome. The account would analyse how the events are linked and this would all be supported by accurate and relevant information.

Points that you could make in your analytical narrative are as follows (highlighting shows where answers would start to analyse consequences, bullets used for convenience):

- In 1865, the Civil War ended and the Texan economy was in trouble: there were huge numbers of half-wild cattle in Texas and high demand for beef in the northern cities. Long drives were organised to railheads in Kansas. For cowboys, this meant round-ups in Texas and then long, challenging drives along trails, with the challenges including stampedes, rustlers, Indian attacks, wild animals, thunderstorms, and hostility from farmers because of Texas fever; the long periods of time away from Texas (e.g. six months to herd cattle all the way up the Goodnight-Loving Trail to Cheyenne); and the outdoor lifestyle: sleeping in the open, guarding 3000 cattle, organisation into outfits, need to pace the speed of the herd, etc.

- Cow-towns: Abilene was established as a cow town when the Kansas-Pacific railroad reached it in 1867. The result for the lives of cowboys: new trail to follow (the Chisholm Trail), which led through Indian Territory. As a result, there was a need to negotiate a fee to cross Indian Territory. Abilene was planned as a stockyard for cattle but also as a place for where paid-off cowboys could spend their money on entertainment. The results of this for cowboy lifestyles: how cowboys spent their money; attempts to control their behaviour; how cowboys tended to spend all their money and then had to find their way back to Texas and earn a living until the next drive.

- Development of ranching on the open-range: linked to John Iliff's first ranch. The impact of ranching on the lives of cowboys: the round up; branding cattle to identify which ranch owned which animals; life in a bunkhouse; ranch rules and restrictions; and drives to railheads now taking days rather than months. Continued challenges: rustlers and conflict with homesteaders.

- Introduction of barbed wire: link to conflict with homesteaders and with sheepherders over use of the open range. Start of changes to open-range ranching in areas with a growing number of homesteaders:. Ranchers having to fence off pastures with barbed wire and changes for the lives of cowboys: setting up and repairing barbed-wire fencing; growing and harvesting hay for the cattle to eat in winter; and patrolling the boundaries of the ranch.

43. Practice

3 For question 3, you pick two out of the three parts of the question on offer, with each part being worth 8 marks for a total of 16. That makes question 3 worth half of all the marks available for your American West exam, meaning it is important to leave yourself plenty of time for question 3 and that it is important to give equal time to each of the two parts you tackle. Since you cannot get any more than 8 marks for the first answer, it is not a good idea to spend all your question 3 time on the first answer and not leave enough to do a good job on the second.

Notes for answers on all three of the parts are provided here, but do remember that you only need to answer two. Also, although we have used bullet points for these answer notes, that is just to make the points easier for you to check your answer against – don't use bullets in your own answers.

(i) Relevant points concerning why the Homestead Act was important for the settlement of the West could include:

- It provided virtually free land in the West for people to settle on (AO1 evidence to back this point up here could be the size of the plots (160 acres), the cost of filing a claim ($10) and the cost of 'proving up' ($30). This was important for settlement because previous attempts by the government to settle public land in the West had not done well, because the plots were too big (640 acres) and too expensive ($640 for a plot) for ordinary people to afford.

- It was open to almost everyone (AO1 points here: to former slaves, to female heads of households, to Union soldiers, to people who weren't US citizens but planned to be, including European immigrants, Mexicans in former Mexican areas, etc). This was important for settlement because the Civil War had created many new potential migrants to the West.

- It encouraged settlement by homesteaders: family farms and individual farmers (AO1 would be information on the restrictions: only one claim per individual, homesteaders had to build a house on their plot, plant 5 acres with crops and farm the land for five years before they could 'prove up'). This was important for settlement because it aimed to prevent speculators buying up all the land and only selling it to the big landowners who could afford to spend a lot of money.

- The Homestead Act led to parts of the Great Plains being settled for the first time (AO1 could be that nearly half the land settled in Nebraska was settled because of the Homestead Act). This was important for settlement because previously people had avoided settling the Plains in large numbers, due to the challenges of farming the Plains. The Homestead Act, and other factors, enabled the mass settlement of the Plains.

(ii) Relevant points concerning why the Gold Rush was important for problems of lawlessness in towns and settlements could include:

- The Gold Rush brought very large numbers of people to California, resulting in large new settlements springing up out of nowhere (with no law and order), or existing settlements that did already have a small police force being swamped by huge numbers of new arrivals (AO1 could include details on numbers of migrants: for example 8000 non-Indians in California in 1846, 120 000 by 1850). This was important for problems of lawlessness because there either wasn't anyone to enforce the law, or the numbers of law officers who were available were far too small to be able to police the huge numbers of people.

- The Gold Rush brought together migrants who would never normally have lived alongside each other, and this led to racially motivated crimes (AO1 support for this could include the 1852 famine in China that led to a huge increase in migration from China to California: from 2000 Chinese, in 1851, to 20 000, in 1852). This was important in creating problems of lawlessness because it increased crimes, including murders, and because the racism of the US legal system at the time meant that white people were easily able to get away with crimes against other races, and people from other races were blamed for crimes committed by whites.

- Gold, and the desire to find it, increased lawlessness. This increased problems of lawlessness because men turned to crime in order to steal gold from those who had found it, or to steal promising claims, or to cheat new arrivals by selling them already worked-out claims. Mining camps often had problems with road agents holding up travellers and stealing from them. Men who were desperate to find gold and were disappointed grew frustrated, leading to increased amounts of heavy drinking, fighting and theft.

- The failure of most of the 49-ers to find gold saw a large increase in the unemployed population of San Francisco, which contributed to the formation of criminal gangs (AO1 information could be that this meant a crime wave in 1851 in San Francisco). This was important for problems of lawlessness because there were nowhere near enough police in San Francisco to stop the gangs, and the gangs were also able to pay off the police, bribe the courts and intimidate witnesses. The lawlessness reached the point where gang members would take whatever they wanted from shops and commit murder without anyone then arresting them.

(iii) Relevant points concerning why President Grant's 'Peace Policy' (1868) was important for changes in the way of life of the Plains Indians could include:

- The Peace Policy replaced corrupt reservation agents with religious men with strong reputations for fairness and justice (AO1 supporting information here could be about the Quakers: the religious group that Grant favoured for reservation agents). This was important for changes in the way of life of the Plains Indians because corrupt reservation agents had been the cause of great misery and hardship in reservation life (AO1 supporting information could include the way agents and local traders had cheated the Dakota Sioux in the long run-up to Little Crow's War).

- The Peace Policy aimed to provide 'absolute protection' for Indians on reservations from the impacts of white development of the Plains (AO1 information here could be that many white Americans believed the Plains Indians should be exterminated). This was important for changes in the way of life of the Plains Indians because it meant that the US government wanted all Indians to live on reservations, and to be prevented from leaving their reservations so as to avoid trouble. Since many Plains Indian tribes traditionally lived nomadic lifestyles, following buffalo herds, through much of the year, living forever on the same reservation was a complete change of lifestyle.

- The Peace Policy was backed by increased government funding (AO1 detail here would be the size of the budget: $2 million) to improve conditions on the reservations and to set up new reservations and move onto them Plains Indians who were still living traditional lives. This was important for changes in the way of life of those Indian tribes still living free: for example, on reservations there were rarely enough animals to hunt for whole tribes to depend on, and instead Indians were encouraged to farm crops to feed themselves, with the government also providing food supplies as part of the treaty agreements that had set the reservation up (AO1 information).

- The Peace Policy encouraged the assimilation of Plains Indians into white American society and culture (AO1 support here could detail some of the ways this was done, for example, Indian children being sent off-reservation to school where they were taught about white culture and not allowed to continue any traditional Indian ways of life). This was important for changes in the way of life of Plains Indians because it made it harder for young people in the tribes to learn the skills of their traditional way of life, meant heavy pressure from the reservation agency for Indians to abandon their old beliefs and become Christians, and encouraged Indians to behave in ways that would not alarm white Americans.

Published by Pearson Education Limited, 80 Strand, London, WC2R 0RL.

www.pearsonschoolsandfecolleges.co.uk

Copies of official specifications for all Pearson qualifications may be found on the website: qualifications.pearson.com

Text © Pearson Education Limited 2016
Produced, typeset and illustrated by Tech-Set Limited
Cover illustration by Eoin Conveney

The right of Rob Bircher to be identified as author of this work has been asserted by him in accordance with the Copyright, Designs and Patents Act 1988.

Content has been included from Kirsty Taylor, Brian Dowse and Victoria Payne

First published 2016

20 19 18 17
10 9 8 7 6 5 4 3 2

British Library Cataloguing in Publication Data
A catalogue record for this book is available from the British Library

ISBN 978 1 292 16977 4

Printed in Slovakia by Neografia

Acknowledgements
The author and publisher would like to thank the following individuals and organisations for permission to reproduce photographs:

(Key: b-bottom; c-centre; l-left; r-right; t-top)

Alamy Images: Everett Collection Historical 26br, GL Archive 26tr, Granger, NYC. 9l, 25, 27, Heritage Image Partnership Ltd 3t, North Wind Picture Archive 2, 3c, 3b, 6, 7, 14t, 14b, 22, Patrick Guenette 9r, World History Archive 16bl; **Getty Images:** Bettmann 11, 16cr, 23br, Fotosearch 16tl, Hulton Archive 1, 20, ullstein bild 19; **Harper's Weekly / HarpWeek, LLC:** 21; **Mary Evans Picture Library:** 8; **Science Photo Library Ltd**: Richard and Ellen Thane 23tr; **Shutterstock.com**: Mikhail Kolesnikov 23cl

All other images © Pearson Education

Notes from the publisher

1. In order to ensure that this resource offers high-quality support for the associated Pearson qualification, it has been through a review process by the awarding body. This process confirms that this resource fully covers the teaching and learning content of the specification or part of a specification at which it is aimed. It also confirms that it demonstrates an appropriate balance between the development of subject skills, knowledge and understanding, in addition to preparation for assessment.

Endorsement does not cover any guidance on assessment activities or processes (e.g. practice questions or advice on how to answer assessment questions), included in the resource nor does it prescribe any particular approach to the teaching or delivery of a related course.

While the publishers have made every attempt to ensure that advice on the qualification and its assessment is accurate, the official specification and associated assessment guidance materials are the only authoritative source of information and should always be referred to for definitive guidance.

Pearson examiners have not contributed to any sections in this resource relevant to examination papers for which they have responsibility.

Examiners will not use endorsed resources as a source of material for any assessment set by Pearson.

Endorsement of a resource does not mean that the resource is required to achieve this Pearson qualification, nor does it mean that it is the only suitable material available to support the qualification, and any resource lists produced by the awarding body shall include this and other appropriate resources.

2. Pearson has robust editorial processes, including answer and fact checks, to ensure the accuracy of the content in this publication, and every effort is made to ensure this publication is free of errors. We are, however, only human, and occasionally errors do occur. Pearson is not liable for any misunderstandings that arise as a result of errors in this publication, but it is our priority to ensure that the content is accurate. If you spot an error, please do contact us at resourcescorrections@pearson.com so we can make sure it is corrected.